OUT ON THE FIELD

OUT ON THE FIELD

Gender, Sport and Sexualities

Helen Jefferson Lenskyj

Women's Press

Toronto

Out on the Field: Gender, Sport and Sexualities
Helen Jefferson Lenskyj

First published in 2003 by
Women's Press, an imprint of Canadian Scholars' Press Inc.
180 Bloor Street West, Suite 801
Toronto, Ontario
M5S 2V6

www.womenspress.ca

All photographs in Chapter 6 were taken from the 1992–93 calendar *Celebrating Ten Years of the Notso Amazon Softball League* and are copyright © R. Hasner. Used with permission.

Every reasonable effort has been made to identify copyright holders. Women's Press would be pleased to have any errors or omissions brought to its attention.

Women's Press gratefully acknowledges financial support for our publishing activities from the Ontario Arts Council, the Canada Council for the Arts, the Government of Canada through the Book Publishing Industry Development Program (BPIDP), and the Government of Ontario through the Ontario Book Initiative.

National Library of Canada Cataloguing in Publication Data

Lenskyj, Helen
    Out in the field : gender, sport and sexualities / Helen Lenskyj.

Includes bibliographical references and index.
ISBN 0-88961-416-4

1. Lesbian athletes. 2. Women athletes. 3. Sex discrimination in sports.
I. Title.

GV709.L44 2003   796'.082   C2003-903691-X

Cover design, text design and layout by Susan Thomas/Digital Zone
Author photos by Liz Green (back cover) and Eileen Thomas (page 174)

05   06   07   08   6   5   4   3   2

Printed and bound in Canada by AGMV Marquis Imprimeur, Inc.

ONTARIO ARTS COUNCIL
CONSEIL DES ARTS DE L'ONTARIO

THE CANADA COUNCIL | LE CONSEIL DES ARTS
FOR THE ARTS | DU CANADA
SINCE 1957 | DEPUIS 1957

Canadä

To Liz, with love

Table of Contents

PART II:

PART III:

Acknowledgements

This book has been about 15 years in the making. Over that time I've received valuable feedback and support from sport sociology colleagues and friends in Canada, the United States, Australia and New Zealand, as well as from those in the North American Society for the Sociology of Sport. Thanks are also due to all the anonymous reviewers who commented on earlier versions of papers that first appeared as journal articles before I edited them for this book. My home department, Sociology and Equity Studies in Education, in the Ontario Institute for Studies in Education, University of Toronto, has provided institutional support since 1996, and my former department, Adult Education, did so from 1991 to 1996.

Professor Jim McKay, University of Queensland, and Professor Mary Jo Kane, head of the Tucker Centre for Girls and Women in Sport, University of Minnesota, kindly sent me newspaper clippings relevant to the discussion of sport media in Chapter 3, and Liz Green provided invaluable help with research and proofreading.

It was a pleasure to work with Women's Press again, and I would like to thank Althea Prince for her ongoing support and enthusiasm, and the production and marketing teams for all their hard work.

Finally, I would like to thank my partner and my children, without whose love and support this would not have been possible.

Copyright Acknowledgements

An earlier version of Chapter 1, titled "Combating homophobia in sport and physical education: Academic and professional responsibilities," was originally published in *Sociology of Sport Journal* 8(1), 1991, 61–69. Reprinted with permission.

An earlier version of Chapter 2, titled "Unsafe at home base: Women's experiences of sexual harassment in university sport and physical education," was originally published in *Women in Sport and Physical Activity Journal*, *1*(1), 1992, 19–34.

An earlier version of Chapter 3, titled "Sport and the threat to gender boundaries," was originally published in *Sporting Traditions*, *12*(1), 1995, 47–60. www.sporthistory.org.

Chapter 3 includes an edited excerpt from "Women in the sport media: issues of gender and sexualities," co-authored by Helen Lenskyj and M.J. Kane, which was originally published in L. Wenner (Ed.), *MediaSport: Cultural Sensibilities and Sport in the Media Age* (pp. 185–201), New York: Routledge, 1998. Reprinted with permission of co-authors.

An earlier version of Chapter 4, titled "Good sports: Feminists organizing on sport issues in the 1970s and 1980s," was originally published in *Resources for Feminist Research* 20(3/4), 1992, 130–136. Reprinted with permission.

An earlier version of Chapter 5, titled "The More Things Change: Women, Sport and the Olympic Industry, 1900-2000," was originally published in *Fireweed* 71/72, 2001, 78–83.

An earlier version of Chapter 6, titled "Sexuality and femininity in sport contexts: Issues and alternatives," was originally published in *Journal of Sport and Social Issues,* 18(4), 1994, 356–376.

An earlier version of Chapter 7, titled "No fear? Lesbians in sport and physical education," was originally published in *Women in Sport and Physical Activity Journal* 6:2, 1997, 7–22.

An earlier version of Chapter 8, titled "Out on the field: Lesbians in sport fiction," was originally published in *Aethlon: The Journal of Sport Literature* 12:2, 1995, 99–112.

An earlier version of Chapter 9, titled "Gay Games or Gay Olympics? Implications for lesbian inclusion," was originally published in *Canadian Woman Studies* 21:3, 2002, 24–28. Reprinted with permission of author.

Introduction

My first contact with Women's Press took place 20 years ago, when I approached them with my freshly minted doctoral dissertation in hand. Not very enthusiastic about a purely historical study of Ontario girls' physical education, 1890–1930, they suggested that I fill in the period from 1930 to the 1980s. A year later, the manuscript for *Out of Bounds: Women, Sport and Sexuality* was accepted for publication. Early in that process, I recall that Maureen Fitzgerald suggested I consider the issue of lesbians in sport, a topic that had received little attention in my dissertation. Around the same time, at early meetings of the Canadian Association for the Advancement of Women and Sport, I heard a few women mention lesbians' experiences of discrimination. I privately wondered why this was important. "How would anyone know if an athlete is lesbian or not?" I thought. Indeed!

One of my favourite "coming out" stories concerns a friend who happened to see her former gym teacher in a lesbian bar. "Oh dear," said the teacher, "I do hope you don't think I'm ... an alcoholic!" In my case, I encountered my gym teacher at a recent reunion for lesbian "old girls" from the school that I attended in the 1950s. Her only surprise came when I gave her a copy of my first book, *Out of Bounds: Women, Sport and Sexuality*. The young girl she remembered hated sport, and was "a bit frightened of joining in." We laughed about our new common ground—both lesbians, both physically active.

Since the 1986 publication of *Out of Bounds*, I've often been asked if I planned to write a revised edition. I hope that *Out on the Field* can be read as a sequel to my early ventures into this area. The chapters in this book were written over a 13-year period, from 1989, when I prepared my first conference paper on homophobia in women's sport (Chapter 1), to 2002, when I completed a paper on the Gay Games that examined the question of lesbian inclusion (Chapter 9). Most chapters focus on lesbians' experiences, interventions and initiatives in university- and community-based sport and recreation. Some, like chapters 2, 4 and 5, also investigate broader questions related to female sporting participation, with a particular emphasis on harassment and discrimination, and on feminists' responses to these social problems. (For a recent analysis of harassment, see Celia Brackenridge's definitive 2001 book, *Spoil Sports: Understanding and Preventing Sexual Exploitation in Sport*). Canada and the United States are the primary contexts for these discussions, with the exception of Chapter 3, which examines relevant events in women's sport in Australia, and Chapter 9, which includes discussion of the Sydney 2002 Gay Games. Chapter 8 takes a somewhat different approach by analyzing portrayals of lesbian athletes in fiction.

I have edited the articles to avoid undue overlap and redundant discussions of theoretical concepts, but, apart from minor revisions and additional examples, they are presented here as they were originally published, often in the present tense (which was appropriate at the time of writing). In this way, I intend the chapters to be read as a historical record that reflects the "state of play" from the late 1980s to the early years of the 21st century—a chronicle of changing times, emerging insights and evolving political strategies. It is unduly optimistic, however, to assume that with the passage of time there have been lasting changes in societal attitudes and practices that have advanced the status of women in general, and lesbians in particular, in the context of sport and physical activity—as this book will demonstrate.

PART I:

UNSAFE AT HOME BASE:
homophobic and sexual harassment

1 Homophobia in Sport and Physical Education: The Struggle Begins

Homophobia: "The fear of feelings of love for members of one's own sex and therefore the hatred of those feelings in others."

—Audrey Lorde (1984; 45).

Discrimination experienced by women in sport in Canada and the United States has been well documented, and the gains made during the 1970s and 1980s reflected the efforts of feminists, both inside and outside sport, to challenge exclusionary, male-dominated sporting practices. However, the problem of homophobia in sport attracted little official attention in academic and professional sport circles during these years. Following Audrey Lorde's concise and useful definition of *homophobia*, it is important to recognize how this fear and hatred frequently gives rise to acts of violence against lesbians and gay men. Given that women as a gender group are already the most common targets of male sexual violence, ranging from verbal harassment to rape and murder, lesbians are doubly at risk, and racist violence against Black women and women of colour adds yet another level of danger (Anderson and Nieberding, 1989; Stanko, 1985).

The term *homophobia* should not be understood in purely individual or psychological terms, although it has sometimes been reduced to these kinds of meanings. Homophobic violence is not confined to random, individual acts. Institutions such as the church, the courts and the educational system are responsible for homophobic violence when, for example, they bar lesbians and gay men from holding office, or deny them custody of their children, or fail to include sexual orientation as prohibited grounds for discrimination (Anderson and Nieberding, 1989; Levine and Leonard, 1984; Rumscheidt and Lloyd, 1988). Along with homophobia, *heterosexism* is a central concept in a radical feminist analysis of lesbians' experiences in sport. Heterosexism is "the view that heterosexuality is the 'norm' for all social/sexual relationships" and support for the "institutionalization of heterosexuality in all aspects of society—including legal and social discrimination against homosexuals and the denial of homosexual rights as a political concern" (Moraga, 1983; 105). Heterosexism remains the dominant perspective of patriarchal culture.

Heterosexuality is entrenched through social institutions such as the nuclear family, through cultural forms such as television and the print media, and, in its most violent manifestations, through pornography, prostitution and child sexual slavery (Rich, 1980). Hence it is appropriate to speak of "heterosexual hegemony" to describe the ideological control on sexuality issues that is primarily in the hands of agents such as medical professionals, educators, religious leaders and media personnel. However, since neo-marxists usually use the term hegemony to mean ideological control by *consensus*, as distinct from *coercion*, the term has its limitations when applied to heterosexual hegemony, which is in fact maintained by force and violence in many instances (Kinsman, 1987; Rich, 1980).

Discrimination, Sex and Sexualities

Since men's control and exploitation of women's sexual and physical labour in the private as well as the public realm is a precondition of patriarchy, lesbian existence—specifically lesbians' sexual, social and economic independence from men—poses a significant threat to male dominance. Regardless of their sexual identity, however, many middle-class women entering a male-dominated field such as politics, business or sport also experience the impact of homophobia. These women may challenge traditional race- and class-based definitions of sex-appropriate behaviour that label independence and achievement orientation as male attributes; hence successful women cannot be "real women," so the argument goes. Some are accepted as "honorary men" while others are targets of sexual harassment (Backhouse et al., 1989). Any form of sexual harassment is, of course, demoralizing and destructive to women. However, homophobic harassment has a particularly insidious effect, by creating rifts between heterosexual women and lesbians, and by inhibiting the development of collective political consciousness and action.

There is ample evidence of the chilly climate confronting lesbians in sport and physical education contexts. Many sport administrators make hiring and firing decisions based on women's known or perceived sexual orientation, and the resulting poisoned work environment forces some lesbians to quit their jobs or abandon their hopes of an athletic career (Baxter, 1987; Kort, 1982; Macintosh and Whitson, 1990; Potera and Kort, 1986; Sabo, 1987; Vance, 1983).

Incidents of sexual harassment and overt discrimination against lesbians have been documented in school and university sport contexts as well as in community recreation. Hence many lesbian coaches, administrators, physical educators and athletes go to considerable lengths to hide their sexual orientation from their peers and employers (Baxter, 1983, 1987; Cobhan, 1982; Kidd, 1983). And, like women in other male-dominated workplaces, many lesbians in sport fear that public involvement in feminist political activities will threaten the fragile coping mechanisms they have developed to deal with homophobia and male hostility (Sherlock, 1983; Zipter, 1988). Given the common equating of feminism with lesbianism in sport administration circles, their fears are well founded (Macintosh and Whitson, 1990).

Lesbians whose work involves school-age children—for example coaches and physical education teachers—are particularly vulnerable to homophobia (Khayatt, 1987). The myth that lesbians and gay men frequently recruit and proselytize from among the ranks of the young continues to be propagated in right-wing circles, despite the overwhelming evidence that the major perpetrators of child sexual abuse are heterosexually oriented men whose targets are young girls (Russell, 1984).

Growing numbers of young female athletes are now reporting that unwanted, often coercive sexual attention, as well as psychologically abusive behaviour on the part of male coaches, is so commonplace that it is seen as normal behaviour (Clark and Gwynne-Timothy, 1988). In such situations young women may fear that their rejection of the coach's advances will result in innuendoes about their sexual orientation, in addition to the possibility of limiting advancement in their athletic career. This is a particularly threatening situation for the lesbian who may lack the required heterosexual "credentials" such as husband or boyfriend.

Heterosexist Bias in Sport Research

Homophobic and heterosexist assumptions in the conceptualization and methodology used in sport research serve to validate the "commonsense" heterosexism and homophobia of the locker room and playing field. The concept of gender-role orientation, which for several decades has been a cornerstone of the research on women in sport, masks the

6

processes by which hegemonic femininity and masculinity are socially constructed and enforced (Connell, 1987). Countless studies pose the hypothesis that women in team sports, nontraditional sports or sport administration are more "masculine" than women in individual or aesthetic sports, or women in traditional jobs. Feminist critiques of gender-role research in sport, dating back as far as 1973 (Ellen Gerber, cited in Hall, 1981), have for the most part been ignored. As Ann Hall argued convincingly in 1981, there is clearly a need for sport scholars not only to listen to this critique and curtail their own fruitless investigations into female athletes' masculinity/femininity quotients, but also to convey to their students that such research is both misguided and dangerous (Hall, 1981).

Some research instruments are more explicit in their heterosexist bias—for example, personality scales that list heterosexuality ("kissing a person of the opposite sex") as evidence of *normal* social adjustment (Edwards, 1959, cited in Gravelle, Searle and St. Jean, 1982). And, as radical feminists have argued, the terms *feminine* and *heterosexual* are often used interchangeably, as are the terms *masculine* and *lesbian* (Lenskyj, 1986; Zipter, 1988). These trends are no doubt a legacy of the 1970s sexology literature that posited "childhood gender nonconformity" ("tomboyism") in girls as a predictor of adult lesbianism (e.g., Money and Ehrhardt, 1972; Saghir and Robins, 1973). This research has been subjected to extensive feminist critique for its circular arguments and sexist and heterosexist assumptions (e.g., Fried, 1982; Lenskyj, 1986), and subsequent studies have reported that the majority of achieving women were tomboys during their childhood years (Hyde, Rosenberg and Behrman, 1977; Schreiber, 1977).

Theories and Critiques

The impact of homophobia on lesbians and heterosexual women in sport and physical education, and the various ways in which women and men in national sports organizations have addressed these issues, can be usefully analyzed in terms of three perspectives derived from feminist theory and political practice: liberal humanism, liberal feminism and radical feminism.

In analyzing the social construction of lesbianism, Celia Kitzinger focused on the contrasting ideologies of liberal humanism and radical feminism. She demonstrated how liberal humanism renders lesbianism a private and personal matter—nothing more than a sexual preference—and thus removes it from the political domain. For example, in one hierarchical model of lesbian/gay psychological development critiqued by Kitzinger, the radical political identity, characterized as "strident" and "rebellious," was represented as the second to last stage, followed by the most "mature" stage in which "integration" was achieved; the "mature" lesbian kept her sexual identity secret and did not participate in feminist or lesbian/gay political activities. Thus, liberal humanist perspectives on lesbianism, characterized by the absence of political consciousness or action, undermined the "radical feminist claims for lesbianism as a major political force" and were "politically inexpedient from a radical feminist perspective" (Kitzinger, 1987; 93).

In a less theoretically sophisticated but equally provocative work on the history of lesbian softball in the United States, Yvonne Zipter (1988) proposed two similar categories within lesbian communities: the jocks and the feminists. The jocks exemplified liberal humanist ideology: They were not politically active, kept their sexual identity private ("closeted") and were in some cases overtly hostile to feminism—common survival strategies for lesbians working in physical education or other homophobic workplaces.

For the purpose of this discussion, the category of liberal feminism is used to signify the approach that recognizes the need for political action on issues such as sex equity in sport but fails to analyze the links between women's oppression and women's sexual identities. It should be noted here that most individual and institutional responses in the 1980s did not fall into any of the liberal categories; the ignorance, apathy, harassment and violence experienced by lesbians in sport were indicative of the more common conservative response.

Kitzinger's research illustrates the pervasiveness of liberal humanist notions of lesbianism as private and personal. Many lesbians, as well as many heterosexuals, agreed with such statements as "lesbianism is a private thing; what people do in bed is their own business." Analyzing homophobia scales, she also noted that agreement with this "private and personal" stance, and with the view that "gays are just the same as straights," is seen as evidence of tolerance, when in fact this position fails to recognize the specific oppressions faced by lesbians and gay men, and is therefore homophobic.

Although Kitzinger avoids making this judgement, it seems fair to say that lesbians who adhere to the liberal humanist position reveal some internalized homophobia—an understandable response to a misogynist and homophobic climate. For women in sport, the individualized liberal humanist "solution" that depoliticizes and privatizes lesbianism is especially appealing. The resulting "conspiracy of silence" relieves lesbians of the need to disclose their identities to colleagues or peers, while it reassures heterosexuals that their discomfort at such personal disclosures is justified. Furthermore, it diverts attention from the political implications of women's primary emotional and sexual allegiance to one another.

In a discussion of bonding among women in sport, Roberta Bennett and her colleagues (1987; 377) claim that "whether or not this allegiance asserts itself in physical sexual expression between women is not the real issue. The allegiance itself is intolerable in a society which reserves the allegiance of women for men." This explanation, although valid as far as it goes, tends to minimize the impact of sexual practice on sexual politics. Whatever the depth of their woman-identification, "credentialed" heterosexual women pose less of a threat to male dominance and heterosexual hegemony than do lesbians, whose (relative) independence vis-à-vis men is sexual as well as social, emotional and economic. From the radical feminist standpoint, freedom of sexual expression is certainly a real issue.

Early Organizational Responses to Homophobia

In the 1980s, at least four national sports organizations in Canada and the United States addressed the issue of homophobia for the first time at their annual conferences: The Women's Sports Foundation in 1983; the Canadian Association for the Advancement of Women and Sport (CAAWS) in 1985 and 1986; the American Alliance for Health, Physical Education, Recreation and Dance (AAHPERD) in 1987 and 1989; and the Canadian Association for Health, Physical Education and Recreation (CAHPER) in 1988. (For a full discussion of developments within CAAWS, see Chapter 4.)

Events at the Women's Sports Foundation's first New Agenda conference in 1983 typified these organizations' liberal responses—specifically, the general desire to treat homophobia as an individual, and hence a private, problem. One workshop, reported in the Washington radical feminist newspaper *Off Our Backs*, is of particular interest. The topic was "cross-sex identification," but this discussion turned to homophobia in women's athletics, and participants produced a resolution in support of lesbians. However, as the *Off Our Backs* journalist observed,

> The women in the workshop ... saw lesbianism as something they did in private ... "Why should people discriminate against me on the basis of what I do at home?" seemed to be the question at hand. It seemed so clearly unfair, and people should be educated about how unfair it is ... The women did not see lesbianism as having anything to do with politics, didn't see how anyone could find it threatening. (Krebs, 1984; 2)

This classic liberal humanist view was also apparent when the same women voted in favour of a pro-lesbian resolution, but against one supporting feminist research and scholarship on sport and gender issues.

At the 1988 CAHPER conference on equity, Pat Griffin presented a paper on homophobia in physical education, which was subsequently published in the *CAHPER Journal*'s special equity issue (Griffin, 1989). (For Pat Griffin's pioneering work on homophobia in sport, see Griffin, 1984, 1987.) One of the CAHPER conference's five equity-related resolutions stated "that homophobia be recognized as an equity issue in physical education and that opportunities to discuss the ramifications of homophobia in physical education be promoted." Nine action proposals dealt with some common liberal feminist themes: educating and sensitizing physical education professionals to the impact of homophobia on equity issues, and establishing non-homophobic hiring practices. One action recommended developing advocates among CAHPER staff and members, a potentially political step that could shift some responsibility to heterosexual women and men. Unfortunately, the word *lesbian* failed to appear in any of the recommendations, and gender-neutral language was used throughout. The use of such language presents serious problems, both theoretically and politically: It may falsely suggest that there are no lesbians in sport; that there are equal numbers of lesbians and gay men in sport; that homophobia has the same impact on gay men as on lesbians; or that sex discrimination and sexual harassment and violence are experienced in identical ways by lesbians and heterosexual women.

Finally, a few comments about the 1987 convention of AAHPERD in Las Vegas, at which a session on "Homophobia and Homosexuality in Physical Education and Sport: Issues in Doing Controversial Research" was inauspiciously scheduled for the last session of the conference. The predominantly female audience was estimated at about 300, a clear indication of the timeliness of the topic in physical education circles, and four papers, presented by Jim Genasci, Pat Griffin, Don

Sabo and Sherry Woods, received a very positive response (Sabo, 1987; Griffin, 1998).

Other organizational initiatives addressing the issue of homophobia in sport included workshops or conference sessions sponsored by the Women's Sports Foundation, AAHPERD, and the North American Society for the Sociology of Sport (NASSS) in 1989, and by the Ontario Cycling Association (Cycling Women Conference) in 1990.

Conclusion

Public discussions and educational projects on homophobia in sport represent an important step toward politicizing lesbian issues among nonpolitical lesbians, and, equally important, among heterosexual women and men. At a more individual and informal level, the time-honoured feminist consciousness-raising group represents an effective politicizing tool. In the course of this kind of work, homophobic discrimination against lesbians is explicitly named and challenged, often for the first time. Moreover, the related acts of giving voice to one's sexual identity and naming one's experiences of oppression are individually and politically empowering for lesbians.

From their position of relative privilege, white heterosexual men and women can more readily challenge the homophobia that silences and immobilizes many lesbians, and it is heartening to note that some of the advocacy initiatives within sport associations have come from these individuals. Liberal approaches to advocacy—for example lobbying for human rights protection—represent an important first step in address-ing homophobic discrimination. However, since few jurisdictions in Canada and the United States currently include sexual orientation as prohibited grounds for discrimination, this is a daunting task. Furthermore, the inevitable publicity and expense of litigation and the difficulty of proving a charge represent formidable barriers. Lesbians who do decide to make their experiences public or file a claim of harassment or discrimination against their employer, coach or professor need the active support and encouragement of friends and colleagues, especially women. Too often in the past, public disclosures of homophobic discrimination have precipitated separation, isolation and alienation of women from one another (Pharr, 1988).

Legislation alone will not alleviate all the problems of everyday harassment and stigmatization experienced by lesbians in sport. More radical kinds of feminist protest such as boycotts, marches and sit-ins need to be considered, and dialogue between feminists inside and outside of sport contexts would aid in developing effective political strategies. The participation of heterosexual women and men in such protests is of course essential. A combination of liberal feminist and radical feminist political initiatives may hasten the day when the existence of lesbians in sport gives rise to celebration rather than persecution.

2 Sexual Harassment in University Sport and Recreation

In 1990, an American psychologist characterized gang rape by university sports teams as "sharing": "It usually occurs with a group of young men with a team spirit, and usually living together. I think they end up relating to each other so intensely even their sexual experiences become *shared* [emphasis added]."

—Quoted in Eskenazi (1990).

The past two decades have seen growing awareness of the problem of sexual harassment in higher education. However, there has been little investigation or public discussion regarding the experiences of university women in athletics, physical education and recreation. Given the substantial documentation of ongoing male opposition to equality of opportunity for girls and women in sport (e.g., Lenskyj, 1986; Uhlir, 1987), it is important to investigate the extent to which acts of sexual harassment contribute to the chilly climate in university sport, and thus prevent women's full participation as competitive and recreational athletes, as coaches and administrators, and as faculty members in physical education departments.

A second compelling reason for consideration of this problem is the tendency for many feminist activists to marginalize sport and physical activity as areas that are so male-dominated, so antithetical to feminist values that it is a waste of time even to consider them. For their part, many women engaged in sport and physical activity have demonstrated apathy or resistance to feminist activism. While the reasons for these trends are complex, they are damaging to women's solidarity and hamper efforts to organize against the general problem of male violence on campus.

Feminist Analyses of Women and Sport

Many insights regarding women's experiences in sport have been generated by researchers and theorists who have employed a radical feminist analysis. That is, their analysis is grounded in women's experience and adopts a woman-centred perspective; it problematizes male-dominated, male-defined social structures and systems rather than viewing women's experience, behaviour, personality or values as deficient; and it gives a central place to female sexuality and issues of male violence as constraints on women's lives across social class and racial/ethnic divisions. Furthermore, it conceptualizes women's resistance and agency as well as women's accommodation to patriarchal hegemony (see, for example, Birrell and Richter, 1987; Stanley, 1977, 1980). This theoretical framework is particularly appropriate for an analysis of sexual harassment.

Radical feminist analyses of male violence against women, such as that developed by Elizabeth Stanko (1985), put forward the notion of a continuum of aggressive male behaviour towards women, ranging from the so-called "normal" kinds of leering and whistling directed at women in the public domain to wife assault and marital rape in the private realm. This kind of theorizing avoids the dichotomy between so-called "innocuous" types of male behaviour ("boys will be boys") and "real" male violence. It explains men's aggressive and violent behaviour primarily in terms of male power over women, which, like male power over children, often takes the form of sexual violence.

Throughout this discussion, following definitions given in the policies of the University of Toronto, the City of Toronto Board of Education, and similar institutions, the term *sexual* harassment will also denote homophobic harassment, which is of particular concern in sport contexts. Female participation in this male domain has for over 50 years given rise to allegations of lesbianism directed at all women, regardless of their sexual identities, who are seen as intruding on male territory. Women's participation in traditionally male team sports, in particular, is (correctly) seen as resistance to hegemonic notions of femininity, which are usually characterized by heterosexual orientation, and conventionally heterosexual appearance and behaviour (Lenskyj, 1986). Furthermore, allegations of lesbianism directed at female athletes deter many women from rejecting unwanted sexual attention from men, or complaining about men's sexual harassment, since they fear that such actions will confirm that they are not interested in men sexually, and hence, lesbian.

Researchers of women's experiences of male violence show that silence is used by many women as a coping strategy to deal with the shame and self-blame that often accompany these experiences (Stanko, 1985). In sport, as elsewhere, harassers have depended on women's silence to cover up their abusive acts, and it was not until the 1980s that sportswomen began to speak out publicly about their experience. Like women working in other traditionally male-dominated fields, many female athletes appeared to grow resigned to the frequent acts of verbal and physical harassment in sport contexts. In his 1990 research study of sexual harassment in American university sport—one of the first published reports on the problem—Donald Lackey suggested that women's feelings of powerlessness generated this apparent acceptance of profane language and intrusive touching by male coaches.

Women who train outdoors and in isolated locations—runners and cyclists, for example—are particularly vulnerable to sexual harassment and sexual assault. Some women change their training and activity patterns to take safety issues into account. For example, 47 percent of respondents to a 1991 *Ms.* magazine survey of women's rape-avoidance strategies reported that they no longer went jogging at night. Throughout the 1980s there was a high incidence of sexual assault, as well as several murders of female joggers (Fein, 1984; Thomas, 1983). Yet in 1978, a prominent Canadian physical education administrator assured women runners, who were (allegedly) concerned about their unattractive, muscular legs, that "by jogging in the right places" their "shapely calf muscles" might attract male attention—presumably "wanted" male attention, in this man's view (Shephard, 1978).

Sexual Harassment Questionnaire

The results of a preliminary investigation of women's experiences of sexual harassment in sport contexts will be reported in the following section. The purpose of this investigation was not to estimate the frequency of such experiences, but rather to let women's accounts be heard, and to begin the process of naming the violence that women experience in sport-related contexts. As Lackey pointed out, the fact that sexual harassment or abuse occurs at all in university sport and physical education contexts is cause for alarm (Lackey, 1990).

The research findings presented here include material from interviews with two female athletes, and 10 written responses to a survey circulated to members of the Canadian Association for the Advancement of Women and Sport (CAAWS) through its newsletter, and to women in the Women's Sexual Harassment Caucus at the Ontario Institute for Studies in Education, University of Toronto. In a short article in the *CAAWS Newsletter*, I explained what kinds of behaviour constituted sexual harassment, and asked readers to respond to the following questions:

1. Have you ever experienced sexual harassment in a sport/physical activity setting? Provide details.
2. Do you know of any other women who have experienced sexual harassment in these settings? Provide details.
3. Have you ever been coerced into having sex with a male coach, professor, teammate, etc.? Provide details. (Lenskyj, 1990)

Respondents were assured of confidentiality and anonymity, and the author mentioned plans to report the results in a future issue of the newsletter. It is perhaps significant that responses to the survey were sparse, even though a number of women expressed support for my efforts to end the silence around sexual harassment and homophobia in sport. As one respondent pointed out, the process of describing an experience of sexual harassment often feels like reliving it, and that is obviously something that most women want to avoid. In fact, in the chilly climate of sport and physical education, women are perhaps more likely to keep their experiences and perceptions private than in other, more supportive contexts within the university.

Violence and the Ideology of Male Sport

A key factor contributing to misogynist attitudes and practices in sport contexts is the adulation accorded the macho North American professional athlete, especially the football, baseball or basketball star. Boorish behaviour on and off the field and convictions for drug trafficking or sexual assault notwithstanding, their public images are slow to tarnish. The same trends are evident in high school and university sport, where the administration has attempted to cover up incidents of sexual assault committed by male athletes and to impose minimal sanctions against the perpetrators, apparently to protect the team's and the school's reputation (Callahan, 1990, Warshaw, 1988). In one of the most infamous attempts, a University of Maryland coach tried to intimidate a female student into dropping charges of sexual assault against a member of the men's basketball team. On hearing this, the university's president merely observed that "the coach had every reason to try to protect his athlete" (Callahan, 1990). And the Bucknell University psychologist's statement cited at the beginning of this chapter speaks for itself.

It is no doubt true, as Robin Warshaw suggests in her discussion of gang rape on campus, that the racist mainstream media pay more attention to sex-related offences committed by high-profile university athletes, many of whom are Black, than those committed by "average" white male students (Warshaw, 1988). However, the number of reported cases is far lower than the actual incidence, and many young women are reluctant to report sexual harassment or sexual assaults committed by campus sports celebrities.

Research in the United States from 1983 to 1986 showed that male football and basketball players in National Collegiate Athletics Association (NCAA) universities were reported to police for sexual assault about 38 percent more often than the average male on a college campus (Warshaw, 1988). A 1987 study revealed that college athletes were involved in a third of the cases (cited in Eskenazi, 1990). A survey of sex crimes listed in the *New York Times* and *Washington Post* indexes for 1989 and 1990 provides numerous examples of male athletes in schools and colleges and in professional sport who have been charged, and in most cases convicted, of sexual violence against women, including several gang rapes.

Public tolerance for athletes' sexually aggressive behaviour towards women strongly suggests that it is seen by some as a "natural" extension of the physically aggressive behaviour of male athletes during the game. Furthermore, the mythic male bonding among athletes is mediated by the kind of homophobia that uses women and gay men as negative reference groups. Hence, if a team member failed to show the prerequisite macho attitudes towards women, manifested in sexually harassing or assaultive behaviour towards female sports journalists, cheerleaders, spectators and other women, he would probably be derided as a sissy or a "queer." Gang rapes by athletic teams on campus are perhaps the ultimate display of misogynist machismo and male bonding.

There are two important implications for the related issue of sexual harassment of female athletes on campus: First, the sexually violent behaviour of male athletes contributes to the generally hostile climate that women in sport experience in the university; and second, coaches and instructors in university sport and physical education are likely to be drawn from the ranks of former athletes, and may perpetuate this misogynist climate unless steps are taken to break the cycle.

Canadian University Sport and Physical Education

Large Canadian universities typically have a department of physical education which provides professional preparation for future physical education teachers, coaches, recreational and campus leaders, sport administrators and fitness assessors. Physical education students usually complete several activity courses and outdoor education projects within the program, but need not be competitive athletes to earn a physical education degree. Although many physical education students participate in intramural and interuniversity (varsity) competition, varsity athletes also come from departments outside physical education.

Interuniversity sport for both sexes has been administered by the Canadian Interuniversity Athletic Union (CIAU) since the 1978 amalgamation of the men's and women's organizations. In the period 1978–1983, female participation increased by 26 percent, compared to a 15-percent increase for males (Inglis, 1983; Vickers, 1982). Yet, based upon figures for 1986, only 30 percent of CIAU athletes were female, and only 40 percent of programs were for women (Dagg and Thompson, 1987).

Universities also offer instructional and intramural programs and recreational facilities to the university community at large. For example, it was while using a university pool for recreational swimming that University of Toronto student Beverly Torfason was the target of sexual harassment, and subsequently filed the first complaint to be processed through the university's formal channels in accordance with the 1987 *Policy and Procedures: Sexual Harassment* (Adamson, 1990). Finally, many of the student-run clubs on campus offer instruction in a sport or physical activity to students and staff. Since universities provide financial support to sport and recreational programs, and build and maintain expensive athletic facilities, it is clear that the physical and recreational needs of students are viewed as important components of the whole educational experience at the university. Hence, it is the university's responsibility to promote a harassment-free climate within sport and recreational contexts as well as in physical education departments, as evidenced by the successful outcome of Torfason's complaint.

Sexual Harassment on University Campuses

Female athletes face many unique situations on campus where sexual and homophobic harassment are likely to occur. Women who are not athletes can probably predict some of the dangerous locations and situations: for example, mixed-sex social events where alcohol is served, or places where there are large groups of male students. Additional factors operate in relation to female athletes who are by definition engaged in activities that men may view as "unfeminine" and therefore warranting derisive comments and gestures. Furthermore, they may be wearing clothes that allegedly convey messages of sexual availability or provocation (that is, according to men who use these arguments to justify their acts of sexual harassment and sexual violence). It is not coincidental that in the Torfason case, women in swimsuits were the focus of the leering. As Professor Richard Hummel, the respondent in the case, said, tellingly, when informed that he had to get written authorization to photograph the national synchronized swimming team in the university athletic centre pool, "I'm just really upset that there are so many things I can't do any more" (Leering case forces limits, 1990).

In one of the pioneering studies in the field of sexual harassment in the university, *The Lecherous Professor*, male university professors were characterized as socially inept and physically and sexually unattractive— hence, their harassing behaviour towards younger female students stemmed in part from their failure to relate successfully to their female peers (Dzeich and Weiner, 1984). Some of the incidents reported by respondents to the survey fit this pattern: A former physical education student at an Ontario university in the 1970s who was interviewed for this study reported that the coach of the women's swimming team was known to have a serious drinking problem, and was often "drunk and obnoxious" in front of students. He was notorious for bum-pinching and other intrusive touching ("hands all over" the students), and for walking into the locker room when the women were changing. According to my respondent, the department's way of dealing with the problem was simply to require him to take a year's sabbatical.

Sexually harassing physical education faculty and coaches do not always fit these patterns. Many of the men in this field are current or former athletes, physically fit, comfortable with their bodies and conventionally (hetero)sexually attractive. Equally important, many fit the macho/jock stereotype—sexist and homophobic (Kidd, 1987). This combination is both attractive and dangerous to vulnerable young female athletes in the university, many of whom have spent their high school days in such single-minded dedication to their athletic training that they have not developed the usual survival strategies of their heterosexually active counterparts. For young athletes who are lesbian, the problem is exacerbated because they have little experience in dealing with men's sexual overtures. For most young female athletes, their sport constitutes the boundaries of their world, and university sport perpetuates that narrow focus and closely controlled existence. For example, a Manitoba respondent reported a coach who "approached" one of her friends in high school; the same coach, a married man, continued training these young women at the university, and kept up his sexual advances. The respondent only found out about these incidents after she and her friend had retired from the sport—evidence of the friend's use of silence as a survival strategy.

The Power Relations of Coaching

The relationship between male coaches and female athletes in university sport is characterized by a power imbalance based on gender, occupational status, and, in many instances, ethnicity, and thus is a likely scenario for sexual harassment. Although this has now changed, there was a longstanding tradition in Canadian physical education to hire faculty who, in addition to their academic qualifications, had coaching certification and experience. Typically, people with coaching certificates are former athletes who have retired from active competition. Hence, the men who are today's intercollegiate athletes are likely to be tomorrow's coaches, and the athletes they coach are likely to be young women, since, in university sport, as elsewhere, men coach men's teams, coeducational teams and many of the women's teams. Based upon CIAU statistics for 1987, women held only 50 percent of full-time and 34 percent of part-time head coach positions in women's athletics (Dagg and Thompson, 1987).

Given the organization of university sport, a female student-athlete may interact with a male instructor in two distinct and conflicting roles. In the classroom she is, presumably, an autonomous learner, relatively free to engage in an intellectual exchange with her peers and the professor. In the athlete/coach relationship, however, she forfeits these and other freedoms. Researchers have shown that male coaches are less likely than female coaches to adopt the participatory style that most female athletes prefer (Chelladurai and Arnott, 1985; Whitaker and Molstad, 1985). In other words, male coaches are likely to be authoritarian; their decisions are final.

The coach's authority, especially when athletes are on tour, extends to areas where non-athletes take self-determination for granted: choice of doctor, nutritional matters, weight gain or loss, hours of training, playing when injured, curfew, use of alcohol and cigarettes, sexual activity, social activity, room allocation and so on. In their 1982 publication *Athletes' Rights*, Mary Eberts and Bruce Kidd documented the ways in which athletes lose certain freedoms as a condition of their contracts with sports organizations (Eberts and Kidd, 1985). These restrictions also apply to many university athletes.

One might expect considerable resistance on the part of athletes, male or female, to the kind of authoritarianism that coaches typically wield. However, so powerful is the notion of "the good of the team" and the incentive of winning that individual rights tend to be ignored. Even the most assertive and independent women rarely question the coach's authority, nor do they challenge psychologically manipulative or abusive behaviour on the part of coaches (Clark and Gwynne-Timothy, 1988; Crosset, 1989). However, it seems that while working for the good of the team is axiomatic, young female athletes have limited consciousness of their *collective* powerlessness vis-à-vis the coach. With respect to intercollegiate athletes in the United States, little awareness was shown of their roles as exploited workers in the university sport "business" or of their rights to unionize and bargain over issues of pay, benefits and working conditions (Sack, 1982). Solidarity in the political sense is a new concept for many of these athletes, and the political naiveté of young women has particularly serious implications for their relationships with male coaches.

Sexual liaisons between young female athletes and male coaches in competitive sport are so commonplace that many athletes see them as "normal" or even desirable for financial and practical reasons, especially if the outcome is marriage (Robinson, 1990). In the words of one newspaper reporter, they're "as common as grass" (O'Hara, 1990). One respondent to the survey, in reference to the track coach at an Ontario university, noted that he "had the odd affair with athletes." I would argue that any coach who has a sexual relationship with a young female athlete is guilty of exploiting his power and authority. Indeed, given the limited opportunities for girls and women to train at the competitive level, especially outside of large urban centres, rejection of her coach's sexual overtures could well mean the end of a young woman's athletic career, and in one case in Alberta reported by a respondent to the survey, this was in fact the outcome.

Homophobic Harassment and Discrimination

Harassment of lesbians—athletes, coaches and administrators—in sport contexts constitutes a form of sexual harassment that was rarely a topic of public discussion until the 1980s. Since 1983, several national sport and physical education associations in Canada and the United States have held sessions on homophobia at their annual conferences. A clear view of the climate in sport and physical education contexts emerged from women's responses to these sessions. They painted a picture that is so anti-woman, anti-lesbian and anti-feminist that most lesbians, whether athletes, coaches, administrators or faculty, remain invisible for reasons of simple survival (Lenskyj, 1991b). Yet large numbers of lesbians continue to be active participants in sport (Cobhan, 1982; Zipter, 1988), perhaps because the same women who choose to lead a nonconforming lifestyle in terms of sexuality also choose competitive or recreational activities that do not conform to hegemonic notions of femininity. Whatever the reasons, there is ample evidence that the women in sport and physical education who are lesbian have to survive in a most inhospitable climate because of the pervasiveness of homophobia, which often takes the form of discriminatory hiring and firing practices (Baxter, 1987; Kort, 1982; Macintosh and Whitson, 1990; Potera and Kort, 1986; Sabo, 1987; Vance, 1983).

One woman's experiences of homophobia in the university context will be used to illustrate some of the barriers faced by lesbians in sport. Sue, one of the two women whom I interviewed, is a talented, all-round athlete and has been openly lesbian for many years. As a first-year physical education student a few years ago, she tried out for the varsity soccer team. She had been warned by a lesbian friend that the coach, a woman, did not let openly lesbian players on the team, and that it would not be wise to mention her prior experience on a lesbian community league.

Three physical education students who had played in the lesbian league and were, in Sue's estimation, very good players, were not selected, and Sue was also dropped at the last cut. Of two equally competent players from another department, one who was conventionally heterosexually attractive was selected while another woman (described by Sue as "big, with short hair") was not. The final varsity team was composed mostly of women who were "only marginally interested in soccer," while many of the better players were cut. Two "closeted" lesbians remained on the team, but they did not disclose their lesbianism, or join the lesbian community league, until after they left the varsity team. Although she had considerable support among her physical education friends, both lesbian and non-lesbian ("everyone knew what was going on"), Sue found the whole experience so demoralizing that she didn't try out for any more varsity teams. At the intramural level, however, she found that homophobia was not a problem.

One of Sue's lesbian friends who was selected for the varsity basketball team also experienced homophobic harassment. On road trips, she found that the roommates assigned to her by the female coach were the most homophobic players on the team. While it is disturbing to see that a female coach was involved in both situations, the harassing behaviour can be explained in part as the kind of horizontal hostility exhibited by members of an oppressed group against one another. As well, it was clear that these female coaches adhered to the male model of sporting competition and valued team success more highly than individual needs or rights. In this regard, many feminists would argue that an entire transformation of competitive sport is needed before the climate will become welcoming to all women, including those who are feminists or lesbians.

The Female Athlete's Body

Women engaging in activities that by their nature attract the male gaze are particularly vulnerable to sexual harassment and exploitation. The young women who participate in aesthetic sports such as gymnastics, figure skating and synchronized swimming are subject to ongoing male scrutiny. Thinness is a prerequisite, not just for performance (since a lighter body can move through space more quickly) but for artistic merit (since the spectacle aspect of the sport requires conformity to hegemonic notions of femininity).

Even in sports where the spectacle is less important than the athletes' objectively measured performance, women's bodies are subject to exploitative practices. In many high-performance and professional sports, athletes have to wear the uniform selected by the sponsor or institution. For example, the members of an American women's cycling team were required to wear black-and-pink suits with a black lace insert down the sides, a not-so-subtle message from the sponsors to the male public that *their* female cyclists were still heterosexually attractive and available. The skirts worn by women in professional tennis convey similar messages.

Feminists would question the very nature of any sport or physical activity that jeopardizes women's health, equates artistic merit with heterosexual attractiveness, and transforms what is ostensibly a competition in strength, skill, stamina and coordination into a contest in "cuteness" and sex appeal. It is noteworthy that (women-only) synchronized swimming and rhythmic gymnastics were introduced into the Olympic Games years before women's judo, soccer or softball. In Canada and elsewhere, trends in Olympic competition have an impact on the funding and popularity of university and community sports for girls and women.

In a growing body of literature on eating disorders among female athletes, sexually harassing and psychologically abusive behaviour on the part of coaches in relation to female athletes' body size and shape is well documented. A high proportion of competitive female athletes resort to dangerous weight control behaviours to maintain an edge over their opponents and to satisfy coaches', judges' and spectators' standards of heterosexual attractiveness (Black and Burckes-Miller, 1988; Ciliska and Rice, 1989; Crosset, 1989; Rosen and Hough, 1988; Teskey, 1986).

It has been reported that even casual references to overweight may prompt young women to resort to pathogenic weight control behaviours, and insensitive coaches may precipitate the problem by public criticisms of females who have not stayed within some arbitrary weight range (Overdorf, 1987; Rosen and Hough, 1988). Some coaches go far beyond "casual" references. In public discussions with female athletes, I have heard numerous reports of coaches who publicly ridiculed and humiliated young women who gained weight, by having weekly public weigh-ins and maintaining a so-called "fat list" of "offenders" posted on the gym wall.

In a pilot study on eating disorders and coach/athlete relationships, Jaffee (1988) reported that while most coaches seemed aware of, and concerned about the problem, only a few coaches reported awareness of actual problems among the girls and women they coached, perhaps because they did not know the signs and symptoms. One of the respondents to the survey was the target of this kind of insensitivity and ignorance.

Robin had been a very successful athlete in high school and was taking first-year physical education courses at a university when the incident occurred. She also had an eating disorder. All students were required to have a fitness evaluation, including a "fat test" using calipers to measure body fat at various sites. Testing was done by a male lab instructor in front of all the male and female students. When he measured this woman's fatty tissue on the top of the thigh—a site that he had explained was difficult to measure—he made the comment, "Oh, you're really gonna make me work hard for this one." In her own words, "I was hurt and upset ... I was devastated." To make matters worse, the lab instructor had used the calipers incorrectly and all the test results were inaccurate. Robin's results were wrongly given as obese. After this upsetting experience, Robin did not take any more physical education courses at the university.

Given societal pressure on women to strive to be ultra-thin, educational initiatives directed solely at female athletes are unlikely to be effective, although Carney's (1986) proposed curriculum of preventive education, starting with Grade 6 students, represents a more proactive approach. Guidelines for coaches have been developed in the professional literature: for example, Black and Burckes-Miller (1988), Grandjean (1991), Johnson and Tobin (1991), Nelson (1987), and Slavin (1987). These include the following:

- becoming knowledgeable about eating disorders and learning to identify early warning signs;
- providing sound nutritional advice for athletes;
- setting reasonable time frames for getting weight and fat levels into recommended range;
- maintaining strict confidentiality and sensitivity in dealing with athletes who may have eating disorders.

More than 50 percent of individuals with eating disorders engage in exercise for weight control purposes, and fitness classes are a likely choice for women. The mandatory "Barbie doll" image of female fitness instructors, especially those on televised fitness shows, contributes to the problem by signalling that fit = thin and thin = fit. Fitness instructors can help women with eating disorders by making it clear that the focus of the class is health and fun, not weight loss; discussions of nutrition and eating disorders in class are also helpful (National Eating Disorder Information Centre, 1988). The hiring of competent instructors of average body weight and the promotion of a noncompetitive, woman-centred approach to fitness would also be beneficial; some good examples come from classes organized by and for overweight women (Barron and Lear, 1989).

Conclusion

The view of sport and physical education as a male domain which women enter at their own peril still operates on many university campuses, and elsewhere. In this "male locker room" climate, sexual harassers are more likely to be reinforced than reprimanded, and women in these contexts may tolerate the constant bombardment of sexist and homophobic comments and actions. There has often been a lack of communication on university campuses between female athletes and organized feminist groups, and initiatives are needed to bridge this gap and to facilitate mutual understanding and collective action to challenge sexual harassment in all its forms.

There are several areas in which university administrations could implement change in order to address, either directly or indirectly, the problem of sexual harassment and sexual violence against women in sport and physical education contexts. These include the following:

- equitable allocation of funds for women's sport and physical activity (coaching, programs, travel, equipment and facilities);
- affirmative action hiring of female coaches, administrators and physical education faculty;
- mandatory education programs related to sexual harassment, homophobia and rape prevention for all athletes, coaches, physical education students and faculty;
- funding for autonomous women's groups on campus to deal with issues of sexual, racial and homophobic harassment;
- free women's self-defence classes.

At the physical education curricular level, electives in women's/ feminist studies and interdisciplinary courses are needed, and analyses of gender, class, race and sexuality should be developed in all sport sciences and social-cultural courses and research. A multifaceted approach of this kind is needed in order to address the complex roots of misogyny in sport.

3 Sport Media, Gender Boundaries and Homophobia

In 1978, when I was a lecturer at the Townsville College of Advanced Education, in Queensland, Australia, a remarkable thing happened. A group of lesbian and gay students succeeded in having a section of the student handbook devoted to lesbian and gay issues.

I confess that, given my slowly emerging feminist consciousness and my thoroughly submerged lesbian identity at the time, I paid little attention to these events. However, I clearly recall a rather predictable response on the part of the heterosexual male department head: "I don't flaunt my sexuality, why should they flaunt theirs?"

Silencing and invisibility were certainly the lot of gays and lesbians, both in Australia and in North America, in the 1970s. Two incidents that occurred in Australia in 1994—the first, a female cricket player's allegations that she had experienced discrimination because of her *hetero*sexuality, and the second, the publication of the *Golden Girls of Athletics Calendar* featuring athletes in pin-up style poses—suggest that, although advances have been made by feminist and lesbian activists since the 1980s, the situation for women, especially lesbians, in mainstream sport has remained stubbornly woman-hating and homophobic.

A similar incident occurred the next year in the United States, when a male golf analyst, Ben Wright, made blatantly homophobic comments about women on the Ladies Professional Golf Association (LPGA) tour. Both the cricket and golf examples involved allegations of "lesbian takeovers." All three incidents, which had very little bearing on women's sporting abilities or achievements, were the focus of extensive media attention—a sure indication of the primacy of "image" issues in women's sport.

In the LPGA example, most of the subsequent commentary supported the LPGA players in the face of Wright's prejudice. Following the Australian incidents, however, there was extensive public and media support for the female cricketer who lodged the sex discrimination complaint, and for the female athletes who posed for the calendar, while lesbians were blamed for damaging the image of women's cricket and critics of the calendar were labeled prudes.

I will argue that the three incidents share important common themes, most notably the manifestation of homophobia thinly veiled as liberal humanism, with an emphasis on individual freedoms and the depoliticizing of individual actions. That these controversies were taken up in the mass media as general news items, and not simply relegated to the sport section, is indicative of the public and media preoccupation with sexualizing female athletes. Moreover, the considerable staying power of the Australian stories suggests that "sympathetic" (that is, uncritical) media coverage resonated with the "common-sense" convictions of many readers. Beneath the superficial changes in societal attitudes, women's sport remains largely an aesthetic spectacle shaped by market demand and (male) audience response.

The theoretical approach employed here is, for the most part, radical feminist and neo-marxist, somewhat influenced by postmodernism. While I recognize that women's modes of self-presentation are not necessarily acts of conformity, and may in fact challenge gendered power relations and subvert traditional rules about femininity, I am more interested in the bigger question concerning the effects of styles of self-presentation on women's social power and social position within sport (Bordo, 1989; Duncan, 1993; Kitzinger, 1987). In other words, I am taking up the challenge of theorizing women as agents while keeping in view the very real social constraints on women's lives.

Putting Homophobia on the Sport Agenda

In the subculture of traditional, male-dominated sport, lesbians are by definition members of at least two marginalized groups: They are not male and they are not heterosexual. Their race or class status may contribute yet another layer of marginalization. While men in sport are usually assumed to be heterosexual, because of sport's key role in shaping hegemonic masculinity in most western contexts, the sexuality of women who engage in team sports or other nontraditional physical activity has long been viewed with suspicion. Because their social behaviour is seen as crossing the line into masculinity, questions are raised about their sexual behaviour: Do they want to be men? Are they lesbian?

Given the public focus on the sexuality of women who venture into nontraditional spheres of activity such as sport, politics or the military, many women in these areas experience implicit or explicit pressure to present themselves in ways that are unequivocally heterosexual. In these contexts, the word *feminine* has become a code word for precisely this heterosexual image (Lenskyj, 1986). On the issue of feminine styles of self-presentation, feminist commentaries of the 1970s referred to the "apologetic" in women's sport, a similar concept to Connell's "emphasized femininity" (Connell, 1987).

With increasing female sport participation and the changing position of women in society at large, women's sport was correctly perceived as a threat to the existing gender order. No longer weak and passive, sportswomen were displaying physical strength and endurance, competitiveness and risk-taking behaviours. Thus, for competitive athletes in the public eye, it became important to send out reassuring messages that, underneath their tough exteriors, they were just like "the girl next door," interested in clothing, domestic pursuits and boyfriends—in other words, heterosexual. The women who were lesbian were astute enough to realize that public approval rested on their compliance with this facade of emphasized femininity. This compliance sometimes extended to "marriages of convenience," according to a retired professional tennis player who is lesbian (Anonymous, 1986).

With the gains of the past two decades in terms of human rights legislation and more liberal societal attitudes about sexuality, there is less pressure on female athletes to emphasize their femininity in these ways. Self-disclosure by an increasing number of lesbians and gay men in public life, whether in politics, the entertainment industry or sport, has contributed to the changing climate. Within North American sport science circles, too, a number of lesbian and gay academics are disclosing, and thus politicizing, their sexuality. However, many coaches, administrators and sponsors, female as well as male, continue to express concern about the alleged "image problem" of women's sport, and to put considerable energy into making superficial changes aimed at convincing the public that female athletes are "normal" heterosexual women. Coaches and sponsors of women's teams often impose dress codes that include revealing uniforms, long hair, shaved legs and makeup. In the Ladies Professional Golf Association (LPGA) tour, an "image lady" was hired to promote a more publicly acceptable image for the golfers, while on some American university campuses, there are mandatory "make-over classes" for members of women's varsity sport teams (Lipsyte, 1995). The homophobic agenda in these marketing strategies is clear. Sportswomen, already seen as nonconforming in their sporting activities, should at least try to conform to prevailing standards of heterosexual attractiveness. According to one supporter of the *Golden Girls Calendar*, the photos were intended to counter the public image of female athletes as "masculine with hairy armpits"; most defenders of the calendar unabashedly supported the strategy of using sex (meaning hetero-sex) to sell women's sport (Harris, 1994).

Such thinking has a long history, evident, for example, in the operation of the All-American Girls' Softball League in the 1940s and 1950s. The short skirts that players were required to wear, at a time when young women were increasingly wearing shorts or pants for sport and casual wear, obviously served a marketing function. Concern about the femininity quotient of these players extended to mandatory "Charm School," and chaperones were employed to ensure acceptable standards. A Detroit player was told she would be removed from the team if she had her hair cut too short, while others with so-called "boyish bobs" were quickly expelled. Even Oxford shoes were considered too "masculine" for the required heterosexual image (Browne, 1992).

Related to the marketability of "feminine" athletes was the conservative ideology concerning women's destiny. Throughout the century, doctors, physical educators and other guardians of hegemonic femininity often voiced concerns that sporting participation was "masculinizing" girls and women, or that girls and women who were masculine at the outset were attracted to sport (Lenskyj, 1986; Cahn, 1994). Either way, female sport demanded careful scrutiny, lest male power and privilege be undermined by a new generation of women whose sporting participation had interfered with their (apparently fragile) heterosexual leanings, and hence their willingness to fulfill their destinies as wives and mothers. A lesbian tennis player, now in her seventies, recalled precisely that line of reasoning. In the 1940s, women of her mother's generation used to whisper about how sport "deformed" some women, and how younger women were "recruited into lives too immoral and unnatural to contemplate." As she explained, her mother believed that "marriage to the first remotely attractive young man" interested in her would eliminate the possibility that she would become "one of 'those women'—and mothers did not then speak the name" (Anonymous, 1986; 66).

Given women's tenuous position in the male world of sport, it is perhaps not surprising that women's sport advocates as well as female athletes have maintained a longstanding silence around lesbian issues, in the words of one commentator, "a silence so loud it screams" (Nelson, 1991). Until the 1980s, even feminist activists paid limited attention to the central problem of homophobia in women's sport, the destructive effects of enforced lesbian invisibility and the negative impact on sportswomen of all sexual orientations. Most commentaries, including those written by lesbians, ignored sexual identity as a social variable. A few took the liberal position that lesbians are everywhere, and that sport is no different from any other area of human activity.

There is considerable evidence pointing to the fact that lesbians have been, and continue to be overrepresented in the ranks of sportswomen (Cahn, 1994; Palzkill, 1990). Most explanations put forward to date shed only partial light on this trend. Some, for example, suggest lesbians choose leisure pursuits that challenge traditional notions of femininity, while others argue that women-only sport provides a relatively safe social context for lesbians to meet other women who are strong and independent, and probably lesbian (Cahn, 1994; Nelson, 1991; Zipter, 1988). Others contend that sport offers an appealing outlet for those lesbians who consider themselves to have always been "tomboys," that is, more interested in wearing utilitarian clothes, getting dirty and having adventures in the outdoors than in spending time on fashion, makeup, cooking and other traditionally feminine, indoor pursuits (Devor, 1989).

It is useful to consider the issue from another perspective. It could be argued, for example, that most heterosexual women, having been socialized from a young age to value male attention and approval, are more vulnerable than their lesbian counterparts to pressure to behave and present themselves in ways that emphasize femininity and heterosexual conformity—hence, they avoid "unfeminine" sports.

This is not to suggest that such pressure is "all in their heads";

there are physical and material consequences, ranging from sexual assault to poverty, for women who resist the lessons of compulsory heterosexuality. The heterosexual women who do successfully resist the prevailing ideology and pursue competitive team sport are likely to have supportive male partners, families and friends, and those who meet with opposition at home will probably find it harder to continue in sport.

Sex, Sport and Politics: Two Australian Examples

In January 1994, in what is now a well-known and much analyzed incident in Australian sport history (and, no doubt, in Australian lesbian history), cricket player Denise Annetts complained of sexual discrimination on the part of the Australian Women's Cricket Council (see also Burroughs, Ashburn and Seebohm, 1995). After Annetts had been dropped from the Australian team, she alleged that she had been the victim of sexual discrimination on the basis of her *hetero*sexuality and marital status.

In July of the same year, sportswomen made headlines again for reasons largely unrelated to their sporting achievements, this time when female track and field athletes posed in minimal clothing for a fundraising calendar for Athletics Australia.

The debates surrounding these issues, as reported in a sampling of Australian newspapers at the time, were illuminating in the ways in which they took up issues of female sexuality. I would argue that the simplistic "other side of the coin" arguments ("It's reverse discrimination," "If it's okay for the Rugby League men ..." and so on) that were commonly raised around both of these issues are responses that deliberately and conveniently avoided a more sophisticated analysis of issues of power and privilege. In the current climate of backlash against progressive social movements, pejoratively termed "political correctness" movements, it is not surprising that these arguments fell on fertile ground, with some conservative white male reporters leading the way.

At the same time, in what appeared to be a rejection of a feminist position that has been inaccurately characterized as "victim feminism," some women's sport advocates portrayed women exclusively as agents of their own destinies (and hence, to be applauded for posing in gold paint or revealing clothes). Given the Australian disdain for "whinging and whining" and the dismissal of feminists as humourless, anti-sex Puritans, this position also had its share of supporters.

Unlike their more traditional counterparts who are simply opposed to women's intrusion on male sporting turf, those who espoused the "other side of the coin" arguments appealed to "common sense" (in the neo-marxist meaning of the term). That is, they grounded their rhetoric in simplistic and unquestioned assumptions about rights and justice, for example, the belief that fair treatment meant the same treatment—"you get the same go, it doesn't matter" (Harari, 1994)—and the fear that the rights of "the 98 plus [sic] per cent heterosexual majority in Australia" were in jeopardy. It comes as no surprise that gratuitous references to the Mabo decision on Native Land Rights were thrown in as further evidence of the alleged minority takeover of Australia (Kavanagh, 1994).

Many of these commentators presented themselves as allies of women in sport; they simply wanted to correct negative stereotypes of female athletes, to promote a "feminine, soft and sexy" (that is, *hetero-sexy*) image, and to raise the profile of women's sport using sex as its selling point. They were concerned about image problems (such as allegations of rampant lesbianism) that might deter aspiring young athletes or their parents, and they worried that human rights policies might not protect the very athletes who will promote this positive public image, that is, white, conventionally attractive, credentialed heterosexual women (Games girls' fund-raising, 1994). A few key facts were thus conveniently skirted: There are lesbians in sport; there are female athletes who do not conform to hegemonic standards of hetero-sexual attractiveness; and female athletes of all sexual orientations suffer the negative effects of sexism, heterosexism and homophobia. Only a small minority of journalists recognized the complexities of the issue (see, for example, Smith and Hudson, 1994; Smith, 1994).

Lesbians in the Ladies Professional Golf Association?

In May 1995, CBS television's golf analyst Ben Wright, subsequently described in newspaper reports as a "veteran" of 25 years, was quoted in Valerie Helmbreck's *Wilmington News Journal* article as saying, "Let's face facts. Lesbians in the sport hurt women's golf. When it gets to the corporate level that's not going to fly. They're going to a butch game and that furthers the bad image of the game. ... Lesbianism on the tour is not reticent. It's paraded. There's a defiance in them in the last decade" (Craig, 1995a, 1995b; Hudson, 1995; Martzke, 1995).

CBS pulled Wright from his scheduled coverage of the next day's LPGA tour and summoned him to a meeting in New York with CBS officials. Wright convinced the network that he had not made these statements. The president of CBS Sport subsequently called the *News Journal* story "totally inaccurate and extremely distasteful," and stated that Wright "is a man of integrity" who "has been done a grave injustice" (Craig and Blaudschun, 1995; 94). CBS allowed Wright to resume his broadcasting responsibilities the next day, and to take air time early in the telecast to renounce the story (Phipers, 1995).

Several journalists (e.g., Phipers, 1995; Finney, 1995) drew parallels between Wright's sexist and homophobic comments and reporter Jimmy Snyder's on-air racist characterizations of Black football players, several years before, that had resulted in CBS firing him. This is not to suggest that racism in men's football was necessarily taken more seriously than sexism and homophobia in women's golf, although it is probably fair to say that the second-class status of women's sport was a factor here. However, in Snyder's case, a video provided conclusive proof that he did make the comments, whereas, in Wright's case, it was the word of an older male golf analyst who had CBS's backing, against that of a younger female features writer from a small-town newspaper. This power difference was noted by two newspaper journalists (Finney, 1995; Sandomir, 1995), and it was suggested that Wright let down his guard precisely because Helmbreck was female, "small-town," and therefore non-threatening (Finney, 1995).

Indeed, while Wright became a household word for a few days, Helmbreck was rendered a nameless *News Journal* reporter in the majority of newspaper stories, although *USA Today* carried her follow-up *News Journal* story (Helmbreck, 1995). In it, she reiterated Wright's statements, reported on the supportive comments of LPGA commissioner Charles Mechem, and matter-of-factly discussed lesbian fans' strong interest in the LPGA, especially the Dinah Shore Classic in Palm Springs, which, according to another source, has become "a landmark of lesbian subculture" (Reed, 1994).

Very few of the articles reviewed here revealed any sympathy for Wright, and many seized the opportunity to ridicule him and to lampoon the entire situation, gaining easy mileage from the infamous "boob" comments (he had also claimed that women's breasts get in the way when they play golf). Several reporters criticized CBS for its superficial investigation and hasty reinstatement of Wright. In a sidebar titled "Wright no stranger to controversy," the *Chicago Tribune* gave prominence to another blot on Wright's record that CBS apparently ignored—namely, his 1991 on-air reference to Japanese golfer Jumbo Ozaki as "the Jap Ozaki, who is striking a blow for the foreigners" (Wright no stranger, 1995).

LPGA players and commissioners, cited at length in newspaper accounts, were the most likely source of liberal-humanist rationales that relegated sexual issues to the realm of the private and the individual.

"What we do afterward is our own business," said Michelle McGann (cited in Ormsby, 1995), while Amy Alcott claimed that "these people out here [fans] don't care what anyone does in the bedroom" (cited in Craig, 1995a; 76). According to incoming LPGA commissioner Jim Ritts (cited in Sheeley, 1995): "I think on the LPGA, as in every walk of life, there is homosexuality and heterosexuality, and I think to the fans ... neither of those things has any impact on why they're out there. I don't think they [care] about their lifestyle."

In "the best defence is offence" category, Nancy Lopez asked, "Why doesn't he [Wright] talk about all the men on the tour who fool around on their wives?" (cited in Rubenstein, 1995). Echoing the Australian "other side of the coin" arguments, she went on to say, "I wonder why it is that men can room together and women can't?" (Hodges, 1995). Thus, Lopez implied that lesbian relationships are in the same category as marital infidelity—not a particularly helpful way to confront homophobia. In a more constructive attempt to address the criticism directly, LPGA commissioner Charles Mechem was widely quoted in the media as saying, "In my five years, I have not had one phone call or one letter from a sponsor or a fan suggesting that lesbianism is a problem" (Reinmuth, 1995).

Not too surprisingly, the *San Francisco Chronicle* was the source of the most lesbian-positive analysis (e.g., Carroll, 1995; Ostler, 1995; Ryan, 1995), although there were other newspaper reports that also gave voice to progressive points of view:

- The issue of lesbianism "is a way for men to keep women in their place," golfer Amy Alcott (cited in Craig, 1995a; 76).
- "CEOs [of corporations sponsoring LPGA] know they have gay people working for them, and I'm sure they wouldn't want their companies defined by the sexual preference of their employees. So they're not about to define the women's tour in that narrow way, either," Steve Ellis, *Golfweek* editor (cited in Markiewicz, 1995; 7B).

- "I hope one day to live in a world in which the commissioner can say, 'Our lesbian golfers, and there are many of them, serve as a shining example for young women across the nation, and any implication that they are injuring the sport is not true,'" *San Francisco Chronicle* columnist Jon Carroll (1995).

Homophobia, Heterosexism and Women's sport

For the person who is a member of a disadvantaged minority, homophobia and heterosexism are often experienced at both individual and systemic levels. Take the example of a white lesbian athlete on a predominantly heterosexual team. She is a member of a sexual minority both in the context of the team and in the broader society. On the team, she experiences explicit and implicit pressure towards emphasized femininity in terms of appearance and behaviour. She is required to wear a style of uniform that conveys the message of heterosexual availability. To avoid constant questions and innuendoes, she has to invent a boyfriend or change the pronouns from "she" to "he" when she talks about her social life. And a similar scenario plays itself out in her other social milieus. She presents herself as heterosexual to keep her job; her parents and siblings pressure her to get a boyfriend; her university lecturers make homophobic jokes; homophobic graffiti assail her as she walks down the street; and when she goes out to dinner with her partner, they are harassed by adolescent males. Thus, there is a certain seamlessness to her experiences of homophobia and heterosexism. Notwithstanding the anti-discrimination policies and statutes that attempt to ameliorate this situation, the individuals who treat her in homophobic ways can probably do so with impunity; moreover, their behaviour is reinforced by institutionalized social practices spanning law, religion, education, family and community life (Fusco, 1992; Pharr, 1988).

Now let us consider the possible experiences of a white heterosexual athlete on a predominantly lesbian team. Despite the odds against this happening, the lesbian majority on the team may have succeeded in transforming the microclimate so that it becomes safe for the lesbians to disclose their sexuality, to talk freely about their partners, children and chosen families, and to present themselves in ways that indicate pride in their individual and group identities. Admittedly, the heterosexual athlete may, at times, feel like an outsider, although I would argue that this experience could raise her consciousness immeasurably, in much the same way as a white, Anglo-Saxon person will experience heightened awareness of race and racism issues if she lives in a neighbourhood of predominantly visible-minority immigrants.

Returning to the heterosexual athlete, let us consider what happens after she finishes the game, packs her bag and heads home. Virtually everyone and everything that she encounters validates her heterosexual identity. She sees male-female couples walking arm-in-arm, and heterosexual images on billboards and in magazines; her friends, family members, even strangers on the street assume (correctly) that she is heterosexual and behave accordingly towards her. Her partner is welcomed to family and workplace gatherings, and male-female couples are the norm in her social circles. And if she happens to be homophobic, and chooses to complain to her family and friends about the lesbians on her team, she will almost certainly receive support for her prejudice. (Conversely, if she tells people about her wonderful lesbian teammates, she is likely to be met with stony silence, if not outright hostility).

In short, I am arguing that there is no such thing as reverse discrimination or "heterophobia." When a person who is a member of an advantaged majority finds that she is a minority in one of her many social settings, what she experiences is, at best, a fleeting feeling of being an outsider, and, at worst, individual prejudice at the hands of marginalized individuals whose bias carries virtually no weight in the broader society. It is precisely this analysis of the relationship between individual prejudice and systemic discrimination that forms the rationale for state and federal anti-discrimination statutes. As has been stated in many court decisions, the purpose behind their enactment was not to protect the social position of those who are already privileged by virtue of their sex, race, ethnicity, religion, sexual orientation or ability; rather, the purpose is to attempt to ameliorate the position of disadvantaged minorities (or, in the case of women, majority).

This is not to suggest that those with power and privilege will not make cynical attempts to use such legislation for their own ends, as in the women's cricket incident and, equally important, in its coverage by journalists who portrayed heterosexuals as an endangered species. In a 1980s Canadian example, a man (who held a black belt in judo) lodged a human rights complaint of sex discrimination against an organization that teaches women's self-defence skills (wendo) to women-only classes. The case was eventually dismissed, but not without considerable expenditure of time and money on the part of this non-profit organization.

A parallel argument can be developed about the sexualization of female athletes for the purpose of raising the profile of women's sport. Just as I have argued that the individual experiences of the lesbian or heterosexual athlete in the examples above need to be contextualized, the same is true for the individual act of posing for the *Golden Girls Calendar*. The popular liberal humanist rationales for the women's calendar—Rugby League men have a calendar; what sportswomen do off the field is their own business; the idea came from the women themselves; it's no different than when models pose for fashion magazines; the photographs are "tasteful"; the female athlete's body is beautiful (Games girls' fund-raising, 1994; Green, 1994; Huxley, 1994; McNicoll, 1994)—need to be situated in the broader context in which coercion and exploitation invariably accompany sexualized images of women. Thus, while it is unlikely that the provocative poses of male rugby players will render them, or other men, (hetero)sexually vulnerable, this is a distinct danger in the case of women.

Men's and women's bodies are read very differently in a society where men as a gender group have greater power and privilege, and where violence against women is a widespread and chronic social problem. Consider, for example, that a woman would probably perceive a man who exposes his genitals as threatening, whereas a man might perceive a woman who exposes her genitals as sexually available. In another example common in North America, the practice of "mooning" on the part of adolescent males is viewed simply as good-natured humour, but mooning by a young woman would not be seen in the same light.

It should be noted that the media debate on the calendar issue was by no means one-sided. For example, the response of Federal Cabinet Minister Dr. Carmen Lawrence, who called the *Golden Girls Calendar* not "the best way to go about drawing attention to women in sport" but indicative of sportswomen's "desperation," was sympathetically reported by Lisa McLean (1994) in *The Australian*. Even the predictable verbal leer from *Weekend Australian* columnist Jeff Wells (1994) confirmed feminists' concerns that, no matter how "tasteful" the image, some male viewers will subvert the intention with the usual objectifying and commodifying of female body parts.

Keeping Up Appearances

Much of the preceding discussion has focused on the alleged "image problem" of women's sport. In fact, there seems to be great concern that sportswomen should not *look* lesbian and, hence, give certain sports a bad reputation, but there is less interest in the actual sexual practices of female athletes who conform to a heterosexual image. (When did you last read a front page story about the lesbians on the national synchronized swimming team?) In the debate about lesbians in cricket, some of the more progressive voices agreed that there are lesbians in cricket but called the whole issue "a distraction" and "not relevant" (Harari and Smellie, 1994; Smith and Hudson, 1994). Certainly, it is to be hoped that the time will come when sports-women's sexuality is not relevant, but avoidance and denial strategies do not serve women's interests in the current political climate.

It is worth diverging from this sporting topic a little to note some parallels to the lesbian "image" question that come from right-wing fundamentalist religious circles in Canada and the United States. Several anti-gay lay ministries were established in the 1990s, for the stated purpose of helping lesbians and gay men relearn and reorient their sexual identities, primarily through changing their social-emotional behaviour. Falling into the traditional stereotypical think-ing that equates the concepts of "feminine" and "masculine" with "normal" heterosexuality, and "unfeminine" and "unmasculine" with homosexuality, these fundamentalists appear to believe that a mere change in homosexuals' external appearance or behaviour will inevitably prompt a more profound psychosexual change. It is not difficult to identify the misogyny inherent in this approach, which implicitly calls for a return to the days when "girls were girls and men were men" and when the rules of traditional male and female sex roles and self-presentation were universally understood and followed, and the sanctions for nonconformity were strong and swift. For example, Elizabeth Moberly, a psychologist associated with reorientation ther-apy, proposed that "masculine sport friendships" in contexts such as softball should be promoted to reorient gay men to more "masculine" (that is, heterosexual) behaviour (NBC, 1995). Similarly, the Life Ministries program in New York included beauty make-overs for lesbians on their reorientation agenda; needless to say, softball is not included in lesbians' reprogramming. Getting new hairstyles, and learning how to sit and how to "feel feminine inside" were presented as the route to a heterosexual identity.

The similarities to the mandatory "charm schools" and beauty courses for female athletes are strikingly clear. As in the sports context, *feminine* is a code word for "attractive to men." As one "ex-gay" woman explained, part of her "reorientation" required a change in attitude towards her own capacities. She gave the example of changing the radiator hose in her car, stressing that her new hetero-sexual identity required that she should let a man do it for her. This is a simplistic equating of lesbian equals independent, and hetero-sexual equals helpless and dependent on men. It is, at one level, incredibly naive to assume that changing the outer trappings of gender identity will have an effect on one's sexual preference. As someone once said, "If I wear crocodile skin shoes, will that turn me into a crocodile?" It is offensive, too, to imply that heterosexual men are only attracted to helpless, dependent women.

However, from another perspective, the emphasis on superficial external appearance, behaviour and self-presentation fits very well with mainstream values in western capitalist societies. I would therefore argue that it is this same conviction about the importance of a convention-ally heterosexual appearance that animated the critics of lesbians in women's cricket and the supporters of the *Golden Girls Calendar.* While not abandoning the liberal humanist position that people's sexual lives behind closed doors are their own business, they point to the "image" problem (the obvious lesbians in the cricket eleven) and the perceived solution (the obvious heterosexuals in the *Golden Girls* dozen). No one, it seemed, considered the possibility that one or more of the *Golden Girls* might be lesbian, or that their modes of self-presentation could be sexualized by lesbian viewers (just as many gay men undoubtedly sexualize the Rugby League men in their calendar). To demonstrate how this thinking plays itself out in another everyday situation, I will briefly discuss a sexual harassment complaint lodged by a male electrician in Canberra, Australia, in December 1994.

Policy changes of the 1990s made it possible for electrician John Daniels to lodge a complaint of discrimination on the grounds of perceived homosexuality with the Equal Opportunity Tribunal.

There was evidence that Daniels's male co-workers called him "weirdo, gay boy, gay bar freak, poofter and poof," according to the tribunal. The most salient behaviours that prompted these epithets included having a "trendy" haircut, wearing one earring and taking aerobic dance classes. Other more conventionally heterosexual behaviours, including having a girlfriend and playing competitive Rugby League, were apparently disregarded by his co-workers (Lawson, 1994). Finally, the fact that he challenged the masculine subculture of the workplace by removing a poster of a naked woman that had offended a female staff member was seen as conclusive evidence of his gay identity—apparently, he wasn't misogynist enough to be straight. This example again suggests that self-presentation is perceived as determining sexual orientation, when, in fact, the reverse is more likely to be true.

Conclusion

Right-wing backlash to progressive social movements has made it possible for many traditional opponents of Australian women's sport to present themselves as reasonable critics, and to co-opt liberal humanist arguments for their own purposes. It is frightening to witness how these mean-spirited and dangerous "slippery slope" arguments and allegations—ranging from the lesbian takeover of women's sport to the Aboriginal takeover of "white man's land"—gained widespread currency and popular support. For these reasons, I believe that sport science researchers have a social responsibility to work towards justice and equity for all.

PART II:

LIBERAL FEMINIST RESPONSES:
one step forward, two steps back

4 Good Sports?
Feminists Organizing on Sport Issues

The familiar homophobic response—a hush, a sharp intake of breath, or body language indicating discomfort—was evident whenever the word *lesbian* was mentioned at early meetings of the Canadian Association for the Advancement of Women and Sport.

Throughout the 1970s and 1980s, feminist activism in Canadian sporting contexts showed a predominantly liberal focus, with human rights issues a major concern. Many women directed their organizing efforts towards ensuring girls' and women's right to equal access to the sport and recreation opportunities that had long been available to boys and men. The structure of amateur sport in Canada was responsible, in part, for the liberal path that most feminist organizing took. Furthermore, many women who were concerned about sex equality in sport were long-term employees of state-subsidized sporting organizations, and were thus unlikely to develop a radical critique. At the same time, feminist activism on sport-related issues suffered from a lack of broad-based support from grassroots women's movements, because of the tendency for many politically active women to marginalize or dismiss sport issues.

Sport Activism and Feminist Activism

Developments in sport activism in the 1970s and early 1980s were taking place at the same time, but not necessarily in conjunction with, other feminist activism that focused on issues such as equal employment opportunity, anti-discrimination legislation, violence against women, abortion rights and so on. From the early days of the contemporary Canadian women's movement, feminists concerned with sport-related issues lamented the lack of interest and support from feminists outside sport. There have, however, been some exceptions to the marginalizing of sport issues. A number of feminist publications, including *Herizons, Canadian Woman Studies* and *Women's Studies International Forum,* produced special issues on the topic of sport and physical activity. And throughout the 1980s, human rights issues in sport received attention and support from such groups as the National Action Committee on the Status of Women, the Canadian Advisory Committee on the Status of Women, and the Women's Legal Education and Action Fund.

The rifts among feminist activists on sport-related issues are somewhat surprising, given feminists' strong interest in the female body as contested terrain, and the political activism that continues to surround issues such as reproductive freedom, women's health, media images of women, women and body image and so on. Paradoxically, it may be this political interest in the female body, in combination with western mind–body dualism, that accounts for some feminists' apathy to physical activity—the same kind of contradiction that in the early years of the movement saw groups of feminists debating women's health issues in rooms that were dense with cigarette smoke. Moreover, some feminists continue to view sport as so male-identified, so contaminated by violence and the win-at-all-costs mentality that it is beyond redemption; their own childhood experiences of organized school or community sport may well contribute to this alienation.

For their part, many women involved in sport advocacy work have failed to take up issues raised by their feminist counterparts outside sport, or to establish links with other women's movements. The two related issues of male violence against women and lesbian visibility stand out as key examples of areas that feminist sport activists have tended to ignore, even though many radical feminists have argued that these issues are fundamental to any movement to end sex discrimination, whether in sport or in any other social context. Their significance in sport is clear. As in other traditionally male-dominated domains, female athletes and women in sport leadership who have crossed some male-defined boundary have long been accused of being masculine, masculinized or emasculating, wanting to be men, lesbian or man-hating. The penalties incurred are frequently violent: sexual and homophobic harassment, both verbal and physical, sexual abuse and sexual assault.

In addition to the general avoidance of sexuality issues, feminist organizing in sport has, for the most part, failed to address the politics of difference within sport, especially sexuality, race/ethnicity, social class and (dis)ability. While it is true that some feminist sport scholars are now addressing these issues in the literature, there is need for heightened awareness of the politics of difference among feminist sport activists.

Feminist Organizing and Canadian Sport Structures

Many developments in feminist organizing on sport issues in Canada in the past two decades have been shaped by the structure of Canadian amateur sport. As in most western countries, sport in Canada has a high degree of government involvement. Since the 1960s, world leaders have increasingly viewed international sporting competition as a political enterprise worthy of public funding to the tune of millions of dollars, and Canadian sport is no exception. Government funds tend to be directed towards those sports and events that are included in international competition. Hence, developments in women's Olympic sports have important implications for domestic programs and policies, even though women's self-chosen sporting interests may lie outside of the high-profile sports featured in international competition.

The Fitness and Amateur Sport Act, passed in 1961, marked the beginning of the Canadian government's active participation in the bureaucratization and funding of the high-performance sport industry. Amateur sport in Canada is controlled by 64 national sports organizations located in Ottawa, and their provincial counterparts across the country. Sports organizations are operated by volunteer boards of directors and paid staff. Not surprisingly, the administration, coaching and officiating of sport is, for the most part, in male hands, even in many of the sports that have high female participation as athletes. At the local level, volunteers are responsible for much of the coaching, officiating and day-to-day organizing in sport clubs and leagues, and it is at this level that female participation is relatively high. Women's unpaid work in the production and reproduction of family leisure should also be taken into account: Maintaining sport clothing and equipment, driving children to games, carrying out first aid and so on. Thus, there is a clearly gendered hierarchy in the everyday practice of sport and physical activity.

Sport, Feminism and Social Change

Given the tightly structured, hierarchical nature of Canadian sport systems, there are limited points of entry for feminist activists. Indeed, the male sport community tends to resist any community involvement of a political nature, as events surrounding Toronto's 1996 Olympic bid illustrated (Shapcott, 1991). Those with vested interests in sport—those protecting their class, race and gender privilege, in particular—are the most vocal exponents of sport as a politically neutral activity. The opponents of the Olympic bid, like feminist activists, are, it seems, the only ones prompted by such base motives as "politics."

One outcome of the high degree of government involvement in amateur sport is that feminists have sometimes found themselves in the contradictory position of receiving government funding to criticize provincial or national sport delivery systems. As early as 1974, when Fitness and Amateur Sport (FAS) sponsored the first National Conference on Women and Sport in Toronto, government money facilitated women's discussions of issues and strategies. For FAS, the impetus for the conference came from the report of the Royal Commission on the Status of Women, released in 1970, which included guidelines for future action by government and women's organizations to deal with the problem of low female participation in sport. The female athletes, coaches, educators, administrators and researchers at the 1974 conference drew up detailed action proposals covering research, curriculum, sport administration, coaching, children's sport, commercial sport, competition and the media, many of which still await implementation.

Women were mobilizing at the local government level, too. In 1976, the Recreation Committee of the Mayor's Task Force on the Status of Women (Toronto), headed by Abby Hoffman (later appointed director general of Sport Canada), identified sex discrimination in community recreation programs and career opportunities for women in sport and recreation leadership. For example, community recreation centres offered arts and crafts programs to girls, and listed cooking, choir, theatre arts, cheerleading and baton twirling as girls' "physical recreation." Some of the recommendations for change were adopted, but for many years (coeducational) drama and cooking continued to be offered as *physical* recreation.

In 1980, the Female Athlete Conference, co-sponsored by the Institute for Human Performance and FAS, was held at Simon Fraser University in Vancouver. Noting that the areas identified in 1974 were still in need of change, delegates began to consider the possibility of a national advocacy organization to deal with issues of girls and women in sport. Following a 1981 planning workshop at McMaster University in Hamilton, the Canadian Association for the Advancement of Women and Sport (CAAWS) was born. Its name was later changed to the Canadian Association for the Advancement of Women, Sport and Physical Activity, but the acronym remained the same.

The following discussion is based on documented sources where noted, and, at the time of writing, on 10 years of experiences and observations in feminist organizing on sport issues. It is not intended as a definitive history either of feminist activism in sport or of CAAWS. Rather, it is a radical feminist critique of selected issues and debates of the 1970s and 1980s in the area of women and sport.

Most of the early women's sport conferences and workshops were held on university campuses and had a high level of involvement by university-based women, including coaches, athletes and physical education faculty. This trend had implications for the social class and ethnic composition of participants—most were middle-class and white—as well as for the kinds of issues and priorities that received attention. Because many participants owed their livelihood to the sport system, broadly defined, the discussion tended to focus on liberal strategies aimed at equalizing access to sport and physical activity, rather than challenging the structure and practice of malestream sport.

Around the same time, women in coaching and sport administration began to organize around equality issues. In 1980, Women at the Ontario Sport Centre formed a group known as WASA (Women Active in Sport Administration) to deal with professional development issues and provide mutual support, and, in the early 1980s, at the National Sports Centre in Ottawa, the Au Feminin Network was formed. The mere existence of such groups posed a threat to many male sport administrators, some of whom actively discouraged their female staff from joining.

The Sex-Integrated Sport Debates

In 1981, women at the University of Alberta organized a National Conference on Women in Athletic Administration at Canadian Universities, sponsored by the Faculty of Physical Education. A major concern at this conference was the drop in the number of female coaches and administrators and women's loss of autonomy as a result of the merger of the Canadian Women's Interuniversity Athletic Union and the Canadian Interuniversity Athletic Union (CIAU). As was the case in the United States after mandatory amalgamation of men's and women's intercollegiate athletics, this was an unintended consequence of policy and legislative changes aimed at ending sex discrimination in sport. As long as single-sex sports organizations operated, there were clear career paths for women in coaching and administration, and successful female athletes and coaches could provide positive examples for girls and young women to follow. Equally important, the control of women's sport was in women's hands; in a single-sex organization, women were in a stronger position to challenge the underlying principles of male-defined sporting competition. The Ontario Women's Interuniversity Athletic Union, for example, developed a philosophy statement that identified self-government and leadership training as important goals, and valued excellence in the sport of one's choice over success in high performance or "marketable" sports (OWIAA, 1985). These arguments suggest a somewhat radical feminist analysis at work, evident in the emphasis on sport organized by and for women, and the implicit critique of male-defined sporting systems. However, it is unlikely that the women involved would have described themselves as radical feminists.

On another side of the debate, feminists argued that "separate-but-equal" was a misnomer, because, for women, separate was never equal, most especially in sport contexts. Blatant sex discrimination in government and institutional funding, policies and programs, facilities, equipment, media coverage, training and competitive opportunities for women lent strong support to this argument. Both historical and contemporary evidence made it clear that women's sport was in fact "separate and second-class."

Women who were critical of the separate-but-equal approach were also aware of the pitfalls of coeducational sport. However, in Canada, the affirmative action provisions of the Canadian Charter of Rights and Freedoms, as well as some provincial human rights codes, allowed for both coeducational and female-only programs, and protected the latter from discrimination complaints by male athletes. Thus, it was possible, and in fact desirable, to conduct a girls' hockey skills course or a women's coaching school, in order to give girls and women the opportunity to "catch up" after a long history of disadvantage and discrimination.

This approach, while in some respects classic liberal, was held by many women who strongly identified as feminists, even as radical feminists. They believed that opportunities for feminist transformation could be found in these women-only settings within the established sport systems. The National Coaching School for Women (NCSW) is a good example.

Established in 1987 by CAAWS and co-sponsored by the University of Alberta, the NCSW was supported by various partnerships of national (governmental) sports organizations as well as by CAAWS, with each organization naming a delegate to the NCSW advisory committee. As well, a working group with representatives from CAAWS, the Canadian College Athletic Association and the CIAU planned the week-long program for volleyball, basketball and soccer coaches. Within the working group, the Feminist Process Group was concerned with maintaining woman-centred values within the School, such as caring, nurturing, freedom of choice and control of personal destinies in the social-cultural context of women's lives, while the Curriculum Development Group worked from the list of value indicators to develop woman-centred programs and methodologies (Bedingfield, 1990). From its inception, the NCSW had an explicitly feminist philosophy and its leadership was in the hands of women with experience in feminist activism. However, most coaches who attended the school were employed in college and university sport, and thus were faced with the task of bringing woman-centred approaches to an institutional context that has decidedly male-centred values.

For women on all sides of the sex-integration debates, there is the central question: What do girls and women want? Like their foremothers in the 1920s and 1930s, some liberal women in sport leadership tended towards maternal feminism; they operated on preconceived notions of girls' and women's gender-specific sport interests and priorities. While there are research findings to support the idea of gender-related trends—girls' general preference for recreation and social interaction, and boys' general preference for competitive and aggressive sports, for example—there are significant numbers of girls and women who enjoy and are highly skilled at traditionally male competitive sports. From a purely human rights perspective, these athletes deserve fair treatment, even if their choice of sport—football or martial arts, for example—is incompatible with a particular feminist perspective. Not all girls and women wanting equal access to sport do so out of feminist convictions, and therefore not all would share a feminist critique of the male model—they simply want access to the same opportunities as boys and men.

A radical feminist approach—and one that was rarely articulated in the 1970s—problematizes the fundamental nature of male-defined sport, instead of focusing on changing women, or changing the legislation, to bring about gender equality in the sporting system as presently constituted. As in other areas of feminist activism, many radical feminists in Canadian sport have worked towards establishing autonomous clubs and leagues that are completely outside state-controlled amateur sport systems. Many women-only clubs and leagues that evolved in the

1980s have an explicitly feminist philosophy of participation, recreation, fun and friendship. Many are also openly lesbian or lesbian-positive, and, like the Notso Amazon Softball League in Toronto, have several hundred players. With few or no links to municipal or provincial sports organizations, these leagues have the freedom to modify the rules of play and to organize the league in ways that give precedence to women's, and lesbians', interests, needs and priorities in sport.

Feminist Organizing: CAAWS

Established in 1981, CAAWS had as its major objective "to promote, develop and advocate a feminist perspective on women and sport." In its early years—the era of (relatively) generous government funding of women's groups—grants from Fitness and Amateur Sport Women's Program and Secretary of State Women's Program provided CAAWS with office space and a staff person, covered newsletter production and distribution costs, and funded local research and action projects, and travel and accommodation expenses for board meetings, annual conferences and general meetings. Women often joked about the "federal udder" on which CAAWS seemed overly dependent, and, as early as 1983, a letter to the newsletter editor expressed concern over this dependence, the likelihood of co-optation, and CAAWS's image as a liberal feminist organization (Kirby, 1983). There were, of course, many local projects and actions that were not federally funded, and CAAWS operated almost entirely on women's unpaid labour. However, the dependence issue remained unresolved and in 1990, when Secretary of State Women's Program cut 100 percent of its funding to a number of women's groups and publications, CAAWS experienced a serious setback.

A somewhat diverse group of women was involved in CAAWS activities throughout the 1980s. While most were middle-class and white, some working class women and women of colour, mostly

South Asian, were also involved. Despite the high representation of Black women in sports such as track and field, there were virtually no Black women active in CAAWS in its early years.

Many active CAAWS members were employed in the sport delivery system at the national, provincial or municipal level, while others worked in university contexts—a pattern that was no doubt related to the predominantly white, middle-class leadership of the organization. For many of these women, CAAWS represented their first and perhaps only formal affiliation with a feminist organization, and it was from this group that questions were most often raised about CAAWS's explicitly feminist commitment. Some of the women with sport backgrounds had long histories of activism in sport and played important leadership roles in the organization. Other women, a small minority, worked outside of sport contexts, but had extensive experience in grassroots feminist groups and were applying their experience to sport issues, often for the first time.

Sexual Politics in CAAWS

Lesbian visibility has long been a topic for debate, mostly off the record, within CAAWS. The cover on the first CAAWS newsletter, dated 1981, was a line drawing of a woman kicking a soccer ball. This illustration prompted a letter of criticism from one reader, who claimed that the "picture of the 'Being?' 'Person?'" was "unrepresentative" and called for a more "appealing" picture, helpfully suggesting gymnasts, swimmers or track athletes (Letters, 1982). In the next issue (Winter 1983), a reader praised the illustration and stated that she had no difficulty identifying the sex of the player—a point that was presumably implicit in the first writer's allusion to the "Being/Person" (Letters, 1983). A review of *Personal Best*, a film about women's competitive sport which had explicitly lesbian content, also appeared in the first issue of the newsletter, but provoked no written criticism.

The silence on lesbian issues lasted from 1982 until 1985, when CAAWS held a weekend planning meeting. Past and present board members were invited to discuss their perceptions of the issues and barriers confronting CAAWS as a national advocacy organization. The results of a membership survey were presented, and one issue that emerged from the members' responses—euphemistically termed CAAWS's "image problem"—attracted considerable attention. It was clear that many women present, regardless of their sexual orientation, found it easier to deal with the so-called "image" problem (tacitly understood to be CAAWS's image as a predominantly lesbian organization) than to say the word *lesbian* or even to hear the word spoken out loud.

Informal complaints, voiced around the time of this planning meeting, concerned the alleged problem of lesbians becoming too visible in CAAWS. References to "the lesbian takeover" were heard from time to time. As a result of lesbian visibility, it was alleged, "good women" (presumably heterosexual and/or homophobic) had been "lost." But, as I observed in a 1985 newsletter article, no one asked if CAAWS had "lost" other "good women" (who were lesbian) because of its failure to address the issue of homophobia within it ranks (Lenskyj, 1985).

One outcome of the planning meeting was the inclusion of "sexuality issues" on the agenda of the 1985 conference and annual general meeting in Vancouver. A panel of four women—two lesbian and two heterosexual—discussed issues of homophobia in sport and its repercussions for women of all sexual orientations. The following resolution was passed: "That CAAWS endorse the inclusion of sexual orientation in the Canadian Human Rights Code" and "that discussion papers on sport, gender and sexuality be brought to the 1986 Annual General Meeting." Although the discussion reflected some awareness of the radical implications of lesbianism, the resolutions focused on human rights and education—both liberal feminist agendas.

Again, at the 1986 conference and AGM in Charlottetown, the program included a workshop titled "Out of the Closet." From this session came the resolution that CAAWS "is opposed to discrimination against lesbians in sport and physical activity, and that CAAWS undertakes to support advocacy efforts to ensure lesbian equality of rights." Again, this resolution took a human rights approach to the problem, although the reference to advocacy suggested some awareness of heterosexual women's responsibilities. The next resolution read: "Given that there are lesbians with CAAWS, and homophobia within CAAWS, the Association needs to address these internal concerns."

A follow-up action from this workshop is of interest in relation to developments in another sports organization, the Canadian Association for Health, Physical Education and Recreation (CAHPER), which was hosting its AGM in Charlottetown around the same time. It was decided to draft "a letter to CAHPER to describe our disgust with their refusal to distribute CAAWS AGM pamphlets with their conference material because of the reference to the 'Out of the Closet' workshop" (Resolutions, 1986; 5). Given this problem in 1986, it is heartening to note that, two years later, CAHPER's annual conference was on the theme of equity, and included a workshop on homophobia in sport which was subsequently published in the *CAHPER Journal*'s special equity issue (Griffin, 1989). Furthermore, one of the CAHPER conference's five equity-related resolutions stated "that homophobia be recognized as an equity issue in physical education and that opportunities to discuss the ramifications of homophobia in physical education be promoted." A subsequent action proposal recommended educating and sensitizing physical education professionals on these issues. However, the gender-neutral language of this resolution falsely implied that homophobia is experienced in the same way by lesbians and by gay men in sport.

For many years, lesbians in CAAWS experienced considerable difficulty in keeping the homophobia issue on the agenda. In the two years following the "Out of the Closet" workshop report, only one relevant article (on the Gay Games) appeared in the newsletter. This was somewhat puzzling in view of the significant representation of lesbians on the board of directors and on various subcommittees. However, like many lesbians surviving in the homophobic climate of male-dominated sport, many of these women were not politically active on lesbian issues, and remained closeted. For their part, many of the heterosexual women were opposed to public discussions because they saw this as a non-issue; lesbianism was a private, not a political matter. Other women—lesbian as well as heterosexual—responded in ways that were unequivocally homophobic: fear of "guilt by association," scapegoating of lesbians for all of women's problems in sport, pressure on lesbians to keep quiet about sexual politics, and refusal to acknowledge the ways in which homophobia hurts all women.

The state played a role in enforcing silence on lesbian issues within CAAWS. In 1987, the Secretary of State Women's Program refused to fund any group whose primary purpose was "to promote a view on sexual orientation." Although this was not the primary purpose of CAAWS, there was ongoing debate about the implications for groups that were lesbian-positive.

With changes in staff and board members around 1987, some of these issues became topics for public discussion once again. An article on the Toronto lesbian soccer league, Pink Turf, was published in the winter 1987 newsletter (McKay, 1987). In 1988, the newsletter collective invited me to write an article on the subject of choice and to link women's freedom of choice on issues of reproduction (the choice to abort) and sexuality (the choice to be lesbian). Approximately equal space was given to both issues (Lenskyj, 1988). Tellingly, the article caused the entire issue of the newsletter to be characterized by some readers as "the lesbian issue." Questions were asked regarding the editors' poor judgement in "letting Helen write that sort of thing." One woman subsequently refused to renew her membership because she was "tired of lesbian issues all the time." She wanted women in sport to "get out of the bedroom and into the boardroom." This classic liberal humanist approach that treats lesbianism as a personal and private issue and dichotomizes sexual politics and the politics of sport shows the dangerous ways in which such assumptions can fuel homophobia and divide women (Kitzinger, 1987).

Predictably, a few more years of silence ensued, broken only by a report of the Gay Games in the winter 1991 issue. Significantly, in the fall 1989 edition—"The Image Issue"—there was no evidence that CAAWS members had ever spent days and weeks analyzing the links between homophobia and "image" or that any of the contributors saw these links as important. The only reference that came close to articulating a link occurred in the editorial, where the reader was asked to compare "the words and phrases you would use to describe two women athletes, a field hockey goalie and a gymnast" and to consider if the choice of words might be "limiting or unfair" (Antoft, 1989). These developments showed the importance of a sense of history in feminist organizing. Without an understanding of the issues and struggles of the past, women's scarce time and energy will be misdirected and wasted.

Human Rights in Sport

When the Ontario Human Rights Code was revised in 1981, Section 19(1) and (2) specifically exempted membership in athletic organizations, participation in athletic activities and access to the services and facilities of recreational clubs from its sex-equality provisions. Lobbying from men in provincial sports organizations was in large part responsible for this amendment, although the government's select committee heard numerous deputations from individuals and groups opposing the change.

By this time, nearly 50 sport-related complaints—some successful, some not—had been brought before provincial human rights commissions across Canada. Not coincidentally, when the amendment to the Ontario code took effect in 1982, there were more than 20 unresolved cases of sex discrimination in sport filed with the Ontario Human Rights Commission. With gender/sport complaints now removed from the jurisdiction of the Human Rights Commission, male-dominated sports organizations were given a green light to continue excluding girls and women, even those female athletes who had qualified during tryouts for admission to the team.

Given the embarrassing backlog of human rights complaints, and the public and media attention they commanded, the Ontario Ministry of Labour set up a Task Force on Sex Equality in Athletics, headed by Toronto Q.C. John Sopinka, in 1982. A number of local CAAWS chapters, community groups and boards of education mobilized to provide the task force with data on sex inequality in sport participation and programs. An Ottawa Board of Education research study provided clear evidence that sport was predominantly a male preserve. Girls had fewer activities and lower participation rates at every age and every type of program, and female teacher-coaches were a small minority (Quirouette, 1983). School board and city representatives from Ottawa and region, and CAAWS representatives, formed a Liaison Committee on Participation in Sport to study sex-equality issues. By 1985, this committee was taking a more community-oriented, affirmative action approach in organizing annual girls' and women's fitness and sport festivals.

The first volume of the task force's report, released in 1983, dealt with amateur athletics in the community. At this level, the government would be able to exert leverage relatively easily, for example, by withholding financial assistance from municipalities and sport-governing bodies that discriminated against girls and women. Sopinka, however, maintained that this kind of so-called "government intrusion" would alienate the largely male, volunteer component in amateur team sports, many of whom indicated to the task force that they would quit if "forced" to allow girls or young women on the male teams that they now coached. Not coincidentally, it was male team sports like ice hockey and softball that had been most commonly targeted in challenges by qualified female players.

This male style of sandbox diplomacy—"If you don't do things my way, I won't play"—had obviously swayed the task force. Sopinka cautiously recommended the administrative rather than the litigation route to equality, by proposing the appointment of an equality coordinator who would have the power to recommend the withholding of government funds if and when this sanction was deemed necessary. The task force's second report, concerning college and university athletics, recommended that these programs be subject to the provincial Code, on the grounds that there were no alternative ways of persuading these institutions to comply with sex equality provisions. However, it was recommended that schools, like provincial sports organizations and municipal recreation departments, should continue to be exempt from the Code, and that the "gentle approach of administrative persuasion" be used instead.

Needless to say, the Task Force recommendations prompted members of CAAWS, WASA and other Ontario groups to express their outrage in numerous media interviews, public forums, newspaper and magazine articles. Therefore, in 1985, the time was ripe for CAAWS and other groups to lend their unqualified support to Justine Blainey in her bid to have the Ontario Human Rights Code amended in order to play hockey on a sex-integrated team.

Justine had been selected to play on the Etobicoke Canucks "A" team, but was barred because of an Ontario Hockey Association (OHA) rule prohibiting girls from playing. (Girls and women were eligible to play only in female leagues administered by the Ontario Women's Hockey Association). Blainey's first application to the Divisional Court was unsuccessful, but in April 1986, the Ontario Court of Appeal struck down section 19(2) of the Ontario Human

Rights Code, ruling that it contravened the Canadian Charter of Rights and Freedoms. The Ontario Hockey Association failed in its appeal to the Supreme Court, and in December 1986, the Human Rights Commission ruled that both the OHA and the Etobicoke Canucks violated the Code by barring Justine from play.

The Women's Legal Education and Action Fund supported Justine Blainey's case by providing counsel for the initial application to argue the Charter points. LEAF also sponsored an intervention by CAAWS at the appeal stage in order to file American case authorities where courts had adopted the view that girls needed access to boys' teams as well as girls-only teams in order to advance their status in sport. As Justice Charles Dubin explained, the repeal of section 19(2) did not mandate integrated sport in Ontario. "In the field of athletic activity, distinctions which have a different impact on participants, by reason of their sex, may be reasonable, if there is a valid purpose for such distinction." This represented a positive development in the general area of sex equality jurisprudence, because it allowed for the possibility of achieving sex equality through different rather than identical treatment (Brodsky, 1986).

Conclusion

This discussion of feminist organizing on sport issues over the last two decades demonstrates the predominantly liberal approach that has been at work, with issues of gender equity within existing sport systems dominating the political agenda. Throughout the 1980s, CAAWS, the only national women's sports organization with an explicitly feminist philosophy, generally remained silent on issues that socialist feminists and radical feminists would see as central: labour issues involving female athletes and women in sport leadership, violence against women, and sexual politics. And CAAWS's links with grassroots movements to develop autonomous, woman-centred sport have been tenuous. Even many of the radical feminists within the organization directed their political efforts towards lobbying for legislative and policy changes to promote gender equity, although in their "other lives" many enjoyed alternative, women-only sport and physical activities organized by and for women, without state intervention.

These trends show the power of hegemonic notions of "sport" as traditionally defined by and for men. Although there have been movements to democratize and humanize sport in many countries throughout the century, this one form of sport remains, for the most part, intact and unassailable. The success of the Toronto Bread Not Circuses Coalition in opposing Toronto's two recent Olympic bids represented a landmark challenge to competitive sport in Canada. For Canadian feminist activists, however, success has been measured by structural and legislative change, increased female participation rates, and a move towards establishing women's committees within sports organizations to ensure that women's issues are addressed. And while some women's groups were affiliated with the Bread Not Circuses Coalition, CAAWS was not. Perhaps the time is ripe for radical feminist organizing on sport issues. Only herstory will tell.

5

The More Things Change ...
Women, Sport and the Olympic Industry

In September 2000, I was one of three participants on a Washington-based public radio program. The topic was the Sydney 2000 Olympic Games, and the other guests were an Olympic journalist from *USA Today* and an NBC sports producer who participated by phone from Sydney. All four of us were women, and we were discussing a forthcoming Olympic Games that boasted an unprecedented representation of female athletes.

Twenty years ago, when I first started investigating sport and gender issues, or even 10 years ago, when I began to examine the politics of Olympic sport, I probably would have viewed this radio program as a symbol of progress for women in sport. Hosted by a woman, the show presented three female authorities on Olympic sport, two of whom had top positions in the sport media business—so why was I disappointed?

Liberal Feminist Initiatives and Shortcomings

As has been the pattern in other areas of feminist movements—both its first wave at the beginning of the last century and its second wave at the end—feminist sport activists tend to be divided, in broad terms, into liberals and radicals. Liberal feminist approaches, which have dominated women's sport advocacy and research in North America, the United Kingdom and Australia, usually defined gender equality in terms of girls' and women's access to the same or equivalent sporting opportunities as boys and men. The liberal agenda called for the removal of policy and legislative barriers that prevented (white, middle-class) girls and women from enjoying the same sporting opportunities as their male counterparts. For women holding this political stance, increased female participation, particularly in competitive sport, represented a major step forward, and there is no doubt that liberal feminist initiatives produced a number of important gains, particularly in the past 30 years when many of the remaining barriers to female participation fell. However, given the tendency to theorize inequality primarily in terms of gender, liberal approaches paid insufficient attention to the links between sexism, racism, classism and homophobia in sport, and as a result the gains were not equally distributed throughout the female population.

In the first three decades of the century, the liberal approach manifested itself locally in the move towards more interschool and intercollegiate sporting competition for girls and women, and internationally, in efforts to have more female athletes and more women's events at multi-sport spectacles such as the Commonwealth Games and the Olympic Games. By the end of the 20th century, the Olympics had become one of the major forces dictating the organization of female sport domestically as well as internationally. The possibility that the male model of sport, exemplified by Olympic competition, needed reforming—or even transforming—was rarely contemplated. It is valid to argue, of course, that since feminism is about choices, girls and women who simply desired equal access to the same sporting opportunities as boys and men deserve that right, and should not be called upon to be pioneers in transforming existing sporting practices.

Radical Alternatives

Fortunately (from my perspective), there have long been groups of women in sport who held an alternative political perspective—radical feminists who called for a new ethos in female sport. In the early decades of the century, the goal of many female sport administrators was to maximize participation: "A game for every girl, a girl for every game." At its best, this represented a rejection of elitism in women's sport and a move towards valuing participation over competition. There was also strong opposition to female sport as a public spectacle. The image of young women in shorts playing before a mixed audience, with many male spectators more interested in players' bodies than their athletic skills, was anathema to these sport leaders, whose position was often criticized, then and now, as overprotective and maternalistic. It should be acknowledged, however, that their efforts to prevent the sexual exploitation of female athletes were based on valid fears that, by the end of the century, proved only too real.

At the same time, the "girls' rules" movement did have some shortcomings. When the rules for team sports such as basketball were modified to accommodate girls' and women's perceived inferior physical capacities, the diluted version of the game entrenched existing stereotypes of "female frailty" by protecting players against "roughness," body contact, risk of falling and undue physical or emotional strain. Class and ethnic biases were clearly operating here. Long hours of physical exertion on the part of working class and ethnic minority women were a lesser concern than the short periods of sporting competition in which more privileged women engaged.

During the last decades of the century, radical sport activism took different forms. Among the more controversial issues that its proponents raised were the links between male sporting practices, which legitimated male aggression, and violence against women; the chilly climate that sexual and homophobic harassment produced for female athletes, particularly the significant number who were lesbian; and the need for new forms of female sport organized along woman-friendly lines. Attempts to develop women-only team sports using a feminist model—most notably softball leagues organized by and for lesbians (and lesbian-positive women)—have had considerable success in Canada and the United States, as Toronto's Notso Amazon Softball League has demonstrated (see Chapter 6).

"Olympic Movement" Mythology

In liberal women's sport contexts today, the mythical allure of the Olympics and Olympians shapes the political agenda in both symbolic and practical ways. Despite the stated goals of promoting recreational sporting opportunities for girls and women of all ages and ability levels, many women's sport advocacy organizations continue to give Olympic sport and Olympic sportswomen top billing. As is the pattern in malestream society, the Olympic credentials of women in sport leadership positions within these organizations are routinely flaunted, with little apparent attention to the chilling effect this practice might have on "rank and file" members with neither Olympic experience nor Olympic aspirations.

In 1995, in one of the early planning meetings of Women's Sport International, much of the discussion centred on the need to eliminate (female) gender testing from the Olympics. The argument that this issue affected only a tiny minority of women internationally and did not deserve such a high priority, particularly in an organization purportedly concerned with the broader goal of promoting mass female sporting participation, was not seriously addressed.

In the year of the Sydney Olympics, stories of Olympic sportswomen dominated women's sport media in Australia and North America, thereby reflecting the longstanding popular wisdom that Olympic sportswomen are optimal "role models" for girls and women of all ages, abilities and backgrounds. This view seems to imply that the major barrier to female sporting participation is lack of imagination. Girls and women simply need to see concrete evidence of female athleticism—preferably a "role model" who is similar to themselves—in order to realize that they, too, can succeed in sport. This approach—alarmingly reminiscent of Nike's "Just Do It" slogan—ignores the systemic hurdles facing girls and women, as manifested in their everyday experiences of racism, sexism, classism and homophobia.

In a city such as Toronto, where recreational centres now charge user fees (and subject low-income users to humiliating means tests before waiving the fee), the playing field has become even less level. Furthermore, in light of the benefits to community recreation promised by Toronto's 2008 Olympic bid committee, it is important to note that there is little evidence from past Olympic host cities' experiences of the much-touted legacy of sporting facilities freely available and useful to citizens of all socioeconomic levels.

Recent developments in women's volleyball demonstrate more of the pitfalls of "playing the game" by men's rules. In 2000, the international volleyball federation (composed primarily of men) decreed that female (but not male) players had to wear skimpy Lycra bodysuits or face a fine of US$3,000. Teams from richer countries paid the fines (and expressed their outrage), while women from the have-not teams such as Cuba's had to wear the revealing uniforms. Clothing requirements for international beach volleyball competition similarly exploit female bodies to sell the sport—and, in the case of the temporary Olympic beach volleyball stadium on Sydney's famous Bondi Beach, this sport exploits the natural environment as well.

Not only the mainstream magazines that target women and sports fans, but also those produced by women's sport advocacy groups such as the Canadian Association for the Advancement of Women and Sport (CAAWS), Promotion Plus (British Columbia, Canada), and Womensport Australia, demonstrated a preoccupation with Olympic sport in the year 2000. Story after story reflected the assumption that there was an unbroken line between community recreation and Olympic competition, and that Olympic sportswomen provided an unproblematic "role model" for all girls and women. In November 2001, for example, CAAWS advertised a Toronto motivational speaking event and fashion show for adolescent girls, to be presented by the "Future Is Female" company, which used Olympic athletes and other elite sportswomen to do the modelling as well as the speaking. The Web site www.futureisfemale.com promoted this so-called "high-end, Olympic quality product" as a worthwhile marketing opportunity for corporate sponsors. For a purportedly feminist organization to endorse a company that objectified the female athlete's body as a marketing "product" was offensive, to say the least.

Comments by retired Australian Olympic swimmer (and "role model") Nicole Stevenson leave no doubt about the primacy of competitive sport over all other forms. "Unfortunately, some of the younger athletes are so amazed by how big and how wonderful it [the Olympic Village] is, they lose sight that they are there for one reason—to compete," she claimed (cited in Bernoth, 2000). One might ask about the cultural celebrations and exchanges, the contribution to international understanding, the festival of world youth, the camaraderie of the Olympic Village, and all the other intangible benefits that are the staples of "Olympic spirit" rhetoric.

After all, there is extensive research evidence from a number of countries demonstrating that girls and women tend to value the social side of sport—the fun and friendship—more than their male counterparts, who are more likely to put winning and beating their opponents at the top of their list of priorities (Lenskyj, 1994a). Programs that attempted to promote friendship and cultural exchange among Olympic athletes have not been hugely successful, largely because of coaches' and athletes' single preoccupation with winning. Former Olympic athletes have spoken of coach and peer pressure to avoid mingling with athletes from other countries; some were even ridiculed for visiting art galleries or reading local newspapers while on tour.

Conclusions: A Personal Note

With the liberal approach to gender equality holding sway in women's sport advocacy circles, a radical/socialist feminist scholar who attempts to expose the seamy underside of the Olympic industry—especially its racist, colonialist, classist and elitist character—is unlikely to be popular. After all, her liberal feminist counterparts are directing all their efforts towards getting more Olympic sports and events for women, increased female athletic participation, more balanced media coverage of female athletes, and more women in coaching, administration and sport media, rather than deconstructing the "Olympic dream" and "Olympic spirit" rhetoric and calling for the complete dismantling of the Olympic industry—as I did in *Inside the Olympic Industry* (2000) and *The Best Olympics Ever?* (2002a).

In the course of this Olympic-related research and advocacy, I've had the privilege of working in coalitions with women and men who are anti-poverty activists, human rights and civil liberties advocates, environmentalists and other grassroots organizers, in Canada, the United States and Australia. Since feminists recognize the importance of making the links between various systems of oppression, I would argue that it is time to make these connections in the realm of sport, most notably Olympic sport.

PART III:

RADICAL FEMINIST
ANALYSES AND ALTERNATIVES

Sport, Sex … and a Woman-Centred Alternative

"It's the only league I know where Doc Martens are considered athletic footwear."

—*Celebrating Ten Years of the Notso Amazons Softball League* calendar, March 1993.

"There's always room to be crazy and silly."

—Notso Amazons collective member, 1990.

This chapter will examine issues of femininity and female sexuality in sport contexts. It will begin with a review of trends in sport sciences research over the past three decades and a discussion of the influence of cultural studies and postmodernist theories on analyses of the female sporting body. A lesbian softball league will then be used as a case study to illustrate how a woman-centred model of sport may provide a site of resistance for lesbians through facilitating the open and non-exploitative celebration of female sexualities.

Gender and Sexuality in Sport Research

Research of the 1970s and 1980s in the area of sport sciences—specifically sport psychology, sport sociology and exercise science—was subject to extensive critique for its tendency to focus on male experience and behaviour and to use these findings to generate standards for measuring all human sporting activity (see, for example, Hall, 1987; Lenskyj, 1991a). As a result, when gender-related differences were found, they tended to be presented as female deficiencies. The distinction between gender-related and gender-specific patterns in relation to men's and women's values is a crucial one. I have used the term *gender-related* in order to avoid an essentialist explanation for such differences. I am suggesting here that gender-related differences are socially constructed, and can be explained in terms of differences in the socialization of boys and girls, different childhood and adult experiences and expectations in the family and in society. At the same time, individuals may resist such socialization, and negotiate new definitions.

When this literature began to acknowledge the gendered and sexualized dimensions of sport and sporting bodies, it was the so-called problems of female anatomy, physiology and reproductive function, and not female sexuality, that received the most attention. For example, the widespread medical concern about the effects of amenorrhea on a female athlete's fertility status and bone density was not matched by similar concern about the effects of total physical exhaustion on a female athlete's sexuality.

The low profile of sexuality in sport research may also be attributed to the fact that sport tended to be theorized instrumentally rather than expressively. As a result of the traditional emphasis on performance outcome rather than process, the physical body, and not the sensual/sexual body, was the focus of attention. Hence, the potential for women or men to derive kinaesthetic pleasure from sport and recreation was seldom treated as a valid research question. However, the 1990s marked the publication of several analyses of the sporting body and the sport–pleasure connection, including work by Brian Pronger (1990) on gay men, Allen Guttman (1990) on the links between eros and sport, and Susan Cahn (1994) on the social role of sport in lesbian communities.

In the following discussion, female sexuality will be defined broadly, in order to encompass a wide range of phenomena, including sensual and sexual experiences, presentations of self, self-identity and self-determination as sexual beings. On the question of lesbian sexualities, some theorists have challenged definitions based solely on sexual practices, or even in terms of sexual practices at all, on the grounds that such definitions reflect static and heterosexist ways of thinking about sexuality and sexual identity. While the dangers of drawing attention to same-sex activities in a heterosexist and homophobic world are all too real, nevertheless questions of actual sexual practices, whether same-sex or opposite-sex, cannot be ignored.

As in the broader social context of patriarchal society, men in sport are seen as sexual agents whose activities need to be kept in check (especially the night before the big game), while women in sport, on the occasions when they are considered as sexual beings, are viewed as sexual targets, not as women interested in defining their sexuality on their own terms. Hegemonic femininity has long portrayed the female body as a sexual asset and a physical liability, and therefore strong, active women pose a challenge to white, middle-class notions of female frailty. However, there are limits to the success of this kind of resistance, since female athletes remain vulnerable to unwanted sexualization and sexual attention by male spectators, journalists, coaches and other athletes.

Gender-related differences in attitudes and values in sport are relevant to a discussion of sport and pleasure. There is consistent empirical evidence from social science research demonstrating that women are more likely to list the social aspects of sport (fun and friendship) as their top priorities, while men are more likely to rank competition and winning as most important (e.g., Battista, 1990; Biddle and Bailey, 1985; Croxton et al., 1987; Mathes and Battista, 1985; Scott, 1989; Tait and Dobash, 1986). This research finding has often been interpreted as a female deficiency; in other words, women need to be taught the *real* meanings and values of competitive sport.

Moreover, there is evidence of bias in the scales used to measure attitudes to sport, because *high* scores indicate an orientation towards competition and winning (see Lenskyj, 1994a). A more progressive interpretation of these research findings would point out the possibility that existing sport opportunities do not serve all women's interests, or even all men's interests, and that sport could be transformed into a more pleasurable activity for both sexes if the social, sensual and sexual pleasures of bodily movement were openly recognized and celebrated.

Sport and Gender Identity

Cultural studies and postmodernist theories have focused extensively on gender identity and the female body as a site of symbolic, textual and political struggle (e.g., Flax, 1990; Grosz, 1987), and this work has influenced feminist analyses of the sporting body (Cole, 1993; Theberge, 1991). Following Michel Foucault's ideas about power, postmodernist critics point out that gender identity is an actively mediated subject position, not simply one that is imposed by external social forces. The sport of women's bodybuilding lends itself particularly well to postmodern analyses, since it can readily be conceptualized in terms of contradictions, disruption of gender boundaries and negotiation of meanings (e.g., Miller and Penz, 1991; Schulze, 1990).

Postmodernists point out that a particular social practice cannot be understood purely as conformity or rebellion; rather, the ambiguities and contradictions need to be considered. Similarly, neo-marxist theorists posit a dialectical relationship between accommodation and resistance to social forces. Thus, the theorizing of women as agents capable of resistance is a necessary step in explicating the complex interactions underlying gender identity. It should be noted, however, that debates rage over the efficacy of various feminist theoretical approaches, especially those generated by postmodernists, in explaining gender identity and bodily experience (Cole, 1993; Hall, 1993).

Analyses of the politics of appearance and body management practices are relevant to a discussion of self-presentation in sport (Corrigan, 1992). Some postmodernist theorists have proposed that women's practices in relation to makeup and fashion are not necessarily acts of conformity, but may have strategic value in the negotiation of gendered power relations, or may represent the subverting of traditional rules about femininity—for example, the wearing of conventional makeup by lesbians (Blackman and Perry, 1990). Such analyses assume that women are in control of this aspect of their constructed femininity, but this is not necessarily the case in women's sport contexts, where dress codes are often imposed by coaches, sponsors or international federations.

Other postmodernist theorists call for a more sophisticated analysis of women's body management practices in terms of their meanings and actual effects on women's bodies, lives, social positions and social power (Bordo, 1989). Applying this analysis to women's figure skating, for example, it could be argued that, while individual skaters may choose to play with the dress code or their style of performance, and thus subvert traditional meanings of femininity, at the same time, women's social position and power in the international figure skating hierarchy remains largely unchanged by such practices.

In relation to the broader issue of self-presentation, the concept of hypermasculinity has been developed to explain an exaggerated masculine style—in dress and deportment, as well as verbal and nonverbal behaviour—popularly termed "macho." In the sport context, this style is manifested in the preoccupation with victory and dominance, as well as careful management of expressions of emotion. In World Series baseball, for example, while displays of negative emotion—anger or disappointment—are sometimes captured by the television cameras, it is a rare sight to see a player smile after he makes a good play. Even the high-fives in the dugout are given with relatively little change in players' expressions.

The corresponding concept of hyperfemininity is compatible with the early feminist sport sociologists' notion of the apologetic in women's sport, that is, female athletes' preoccupation with clothes and jewellery, frequent references to male partners and avowals of interest in stereotypical hobbies. With recent changes in legislation and public attitudes, many female athletes no longer resort to hyper-feminine self-presentation in order to assert their heterosexual identity in the face of homophobic innuendoes. On the other hand, there is also the possibility for lesbian athletes to subvert conventional views of femininity by adopting a hyperfeminine style.

Self-disclosure by an increasing number of lesbians in public life—for example, k.d. lang and Martina Navratilova—has contributed to the more liberal climate, although this does not necessarily signify safety or acceptance for all lesbians in sport. The so-called image of women's sport continues to concern many coaches, administrators and sponsors, female as well as male. In one example provided by a Canadian colleague, a male coach of a women's university volleyball team in British Columbia required all players to grow their hair and wear it in a ponytail, tied up with ribbons. This hyperfeminine image is seen as an effective marketing strategy for female sport.

Another relevant aspect of women's self-presentation in sport involves facial expressions. There are some physical activities where it is acceptable, even desirable, for the female athlete to convey the impression that she finds pleasure in performing—that she experiences kinesthetic enjoyment while she skates or dances, for example. And, not coincidentally, it is in activities such as figure skating, gymnastics and synchronized swimming that a highly sexualized, often flirtatious presentation of self has become a prerequisite for success. However, the athlete's smile is simply part of the act, and not necessarily an indication of enjoyment. Indeed, given the intense physical exertion required of these skaters, gymnasts and swimmers, a more appropriate expression might be one of pain and effort rather than pleasure. This is not to suggest that the athlete derives no pleasure or satisfaction from her performance, but rather to draw attention to the constraints on most female athletes' self-presentation.

The illusion of effortlessness in female aesthetic activities is central to their entertainment quotient, and the success of this illusion is in part dependent upon athletes and spectators maintaining a conspiracy of silence, broken only occasionally when the television camera captures a contradictory emotion on an athlete's face. Yet, despite the popular image of smiling women effortlessly performing activities to which their bodies are naturally suited, these aesthetic sports have lower status and career potential than most men's sport. It is therefore ironic that such activities were developed historically by and for women, in part because the more flexible female body is generally well suited to activities requiring grace and agility. At the same time, their popularity is largely dependent on the participants' conventional heterosexual attractiveness, which is itself a class- and race-specific construct. The co-optation of such sports casts serious doubt on the effectiveness of liberal initiatives to produce equity in women's sport.

Lesbians and Sport

Although it is clear that lesbians are marginalized in the culture of traditional, male-dominated sport, an argument could also be made that lesbians occupy a central place in sport, because both lesbianism and female sporting participation share common ground as activities that are incompatible with notions of hegemonic femininity. Sport has traditionally been viewed as a stronghold of hegemonic, hetero-sexual masculinity: Sport is what makes a boy into a man. (Hence gay men are clearly a marginalized group because they subvert this objec-tive; all the sport in the world will not make them into *real* men.) But sport is not perceived as a central component of female socialization into womanhood; sport is not what makes girls into women. On the contrary, if one accepts the vast volume of social psychology research on the subject, sport makes girls into *conflicted* women.

However, since femininity and athleticism are products of social construction, they should be amenable to redefinition. For over two decades, feminists have been attempting, with some success, to trans-form and recreate what it means to be female and athlete. Attributes such as physical strength, muscular development, risk-taking behav-iour and a sense of ease and comfort with one's body and one's phys-icality are entirely compatible with these new and liberating ways of presenting oneself, unapologetically and unequivocally, as female.

In light of the progress feminists have already made towards trans-forming hegemonic notions of femininity and athleticism, it could be argued that sport would be a comfortable and appropriate context for most lesbians, and that heterosexual women might be the ones who experience marginalization in a setting that consciously rejects traditional definitions of femininity (see Chapter 3). In reality, sport is not necessarily a safe and comfortable place for lesbians, nor do all women's sporting practices necessarily challenge hegemonic femi-ninity. Lesbians continue to be stigmatized, sexually harassed and silenced in sport contexts, and women's sport continues to be co-opted, controlled and exploited in the interests of patriarchal hege-mony. Despite the high representation of lesbians—in some sports, a majority—lesbian marginalization and invisibility continue to char-acterize women's sport.

Lesbian invisibility in feminist and other progressive sport research contributes to the overall problem. Some commentaries take the liberal position that lesbians are everywhere, and that sport is no different to any other area of human activity, while others simply ignore sexual identity as a social variable. Reflecting the former position, a 1982 publication explained it this way:

> It is a commonly held belief that many women athletes are lesbians. No one questions the fact that some women athletes, like some non-athletes, are lesbians. To our knowledge, no one has done a head count; nor should anyone bother. For some, the world of sport is considered a sort of fantasy land where all males are heterosexual and all females homosexual. Such views are clearly nonsensical. (Hall and Richardson, 1982; 81)

If a head count were to be taken, in sport or in any other social institution (if and when it ever becomes safe for lesbians to self-disclose), such a statistic would no doubt cause considerable surprise.

Gender Identification and the Limits of Role Theory

Given the longstanding practice in the western world of dividing sporting activities into masculine and feminine, it might be predicted that lesbians would choose feminine sports because they offer relative safety from homophobic suspicions about sexual orientation. Such sporting activities are perceived to be appropriate for (heterosexual) women and conducive to heterosexual attractiveness—figure skating or dance exercise, for example. In contrast, female participants in team sports and other traditionally male activities are often subject to homophobic innuendoes, because they have overstepped some man-made boundary between gender-appropriate activities for men and for women. Yet, although it is difficult to substantiate empirically because of the risks attached to self-disclosing, anecdotal evidence provides some support for the proposal that lesbian participation in

team sports, martial arts and other traditionally male sports is relatively high, and that their involvement in conventionally feminine
activities is relatively low (see, for example, Palzkill, 1990).

The social construction of the boundary between masculine and
feminine involves a deliberate blurring of the distinctions between
gender and sexual orientation, as well as a blatantly circular way of
arguing. In this line of thought, feminine women are assumed to be
heterosexual because they behave and present themselves in a way
that men judge to be conventionally attractive and appropriate for
heterosexual women. Unfeminine (or masculine, or mannish)
women must be lesbian, so the argument goes, because they behave
and present themselves in a way that men judge to be inappropriate
and unattractive. Thus, the characteristics of femininity are socially
constructed from a white, middle-class stereotype of female heterosexual attractiveness. Ironically, many famous media icons of heterosexual femininity and beauty have subsequently proven to be lesbian
or bisexual—Greta Garbo, for example—thus seriously undermin-
ing the equation.

The simplistic equating of gender identification and sexual orientation, and the manifestations of homophobia that it generates, is
practised not only by the uninformed person in the street. Researchers
in social psychology have been responsible for much of the entrenching of this equation. For about three decades, sport psychologists have
been preoccupied with investigating the sex-role orientation of female
athletes and the problems of role conflict and loss of femininity
allegedly experienced by the unfortunate women who have to choose
between being an athlete and being a real woman. Significantly, it is
not the sex-role orientation of ballet dancers or synchronized swimmers that commands these researchers' attention, but rather that of
women in sport administration, team sports, martial arts and so on—
in other words, the women whose sex-role orientation is immediately
problematized because their activities fall outside the boundaries of

hegemonic femininity (see, for example, Pedersen and Kono, 1990; Wrisberg, 1990). Despite a substantial body of literature critiquing this line of inquiry, including Hall's definitive 1981 monograph on the subject, this misogynist and homophobic research continues to be produced and reproduced (Connell, 1987; Hall, 1981).

Although I strongly endorse Hall's and others' critiques of sport research based on role theory, this is not to suggest that these and related issues are not worthy of sport scholars' attention. For example, the view of oneself as an outsider, shared by many lesbians and sportswomen, and entrenched by homophobic and misogynist attitudes and practices within malestream sport, needs to be investigated and theorized in woman-centred, lesbian-positive ways. The following statement, reflecting one lesbian's childhood experiences, captures the problem:

> Gym classes were segregated ... I would play with the girls and they always said that I played too rough. They said I could play with the girls with my left hand only, or play with the boys. So, of course, I decided to play with the boys ... so we're in the gym one day and all the girls were lined up against the wall and there I was alone with the boys playing 'scatter-dodge'. The girls were really cheering for me and I had this really mixed thing that has stayed with me ever since. I wanted to wipe out every boy in that group and I did, by the way—I won. I was the last person standing. I wanted to win for them, for the girls, for them to see that it could be done. At the same time, what was mixed up with this was this incredible contempt for the girls because they were all in their little dresses and little shoes sitting passively on the side, cheering for me, and I didn't want to be one of them and yet I knew I was one of them. (Whitfield, 1986)

This story exemplifies some of the contradictions for lesbians in sport, in a way that is far more complex than the static notions of role conflict or feminine sex-role orientation. This girl had internalized some of the contempt that the boys held for their female peers, and certainly in this context their passivity and their way of presenting themselves (little dresses ... little shoes) was not likely to inspire the admiration of a spunky, active, athletically talented girl. She didn't want to be identified with girls as the losing side (in the game, and in life), although she knew this was inevitable. At the same time, she didn't want to *be* a boy. She simply wanted to be strong, active, competent, tough, and she wished the other girls were the same. And she was determined to beat the boys at their own game, not necessarily for all time, but definitely for this particular game, because of its symbolic significance.

The uncritical use of concepts derived from role theory also undermines a transformative feminist agenda in sport research and sporting practice. The concept of role model is popular in liberal circles as a central feature of equity research and programs, as if the presence of a few women or Black people will undo centuries of discrimination and oppression. This simplistic approach relies on quantitative research showing that there are not enough women in a particular sport context, and that the appointment of a few key role models (for example, Olympic athletes) will demonstrate to girls and women that they, too, can aspire to these heights. At a time when many progressive observers (for example, Justice Charles Dubin, who chaired the Canadian inquiry into steroid use among Olympic track and field athletes) share the view that a critique of competitive sport is long overdue, adherents of the role model approach do not consider the ways in which current competitive sporting practices do not meet many women's priorities and interests, and may in fact alienate potential participants of both sexes (Dubin, 1990).

Needless to say, a woman who is perceived as radical, feminist and/or lesbian is hardly likely to qualify as the ideal role model to inspire a generation of young sportswomen. Retired Australian tennis player Margaret Court was probably voicing the unspoken views of many homophobic women and men when she called Navratilova an inappropriate role model. According to this line of thinking, the ideal role model needs to be a woman who has successfully combined femininity and athleticism, preferably a credentialed heterosexual woman.

The presence of highly visible role models may enhance an institution's image and lessen its responsibility to undertake the structural change needed to address such pervasive problems as racist, sexist and homophobic harassment. It is significant that many retired female athletes—the potential role models—are now disclosing their experiences of the brutality of competitive sport, including abusive coaches, steroid use and eating disorders, to mainstream sports journalists (Christie, 1992; Ormsby, 1992; Ryman, 1992), but very few, even now, are publicly discussing their experiences as lesbians in sport. Apart from the well-known biographies of Billie Jean King and Martina Navratilova, one notable exception is Betty Baxter, a Canadian lesbian activist, former Olympic volleyball player and national coach (see, for example, Baxter, 1987; Morrison, 1991). This pattern suggests that although women have broken many of the silences around the violence they have experienced in sport, it is not yet safe for all lesbians.

A Woman-Centred Alternative

Lesbian sporting leagues organized on feminist principles provide one example of the potential for sport to be reclaimed in the interests of pleasure (Birrell and Richter, 1987; Zipter, 1988). The feminist principles of sport leadership adopted by these leagues may include, but are not limited to, the following:

- Projecting a feeling of safety or security for participants; avoiding situations which generate unequal relationships and may sabotage the goal of cooperation;
- providing women with choices regarding participation;
- avoiding a success/failure approach to challenges;

- promoting shared decision-making and collectivity (Mitten, 1985).

With this shift from an instrumental, goal-oriented to an expressive, process-oriented approach, there is the potential for woman-centred sporting practices to include the celebration of female physicality and sexuality. However, this is not to suggest that biology is responsible for the cooperative ethos of such sporting endeavours. Indeed, as Yvonne Zipter points out in her book on lesbian softball, philosophies range from "winning is everything" to "playing one's best is what counts" to "having fun is all that matters"—and a myriad of combinations. It is not the players' biological identity, but rather a deliberate effort to change sports so that they do reflect women's lives (Zipter, 1988; 115) that is responsible for the feminist agendas of many softball leagues.

The Notso Amazons Softball League began in Toronto in 1984 as a women-only, recreational league for lesbians and lesbian-positive women, organized on feminist principles. I will draw on participant observations as a player and spectator in this league for four years (1984–1987), as well as interviews with two collective members.

Unlike some lesbian teams that operated within mainstream leagues, the Notsos did not have men involved as coaches, officials or administrators, and the league was not associated with provincial or national softball associations. One consequence of this autonomy was that it could not officially compete with other women's leagues. However, since its goal was purely recreational, and since there were usually 20 to 30 Notso teams, there was no pressing need to pursue outside competitive opportunities. Furthermore, it was always possible for the more competitive or talented players to put together a team to compete in the Gay Games, which were organized on the principle of inclusiveness and had no formal requirements regarding recognition by mainstream sport governing bodies (see Chapter 9).

The Notsos were organized explicitly on feminist principles of cooperation and non-competitiveness. Registration forms included information on players' skill levels and preferred positions, and this information was computerized to produce balanced teams. Other provisions aimed at enhancing participation and fun included rules to prevent collisions; safety bases at first base; a rule calling for players to play a minimum of three innings per game; and removal or suspension of any player who acted in an unsportswomanlike or dangerous manner. Pre-season workshops were conducted by collective members and other volunteers, and teams could organize mid-week practices, although there was some debate over the number of practices beyond which a team could become too competitive.

Members of the founding collective stressed the recreational and social aspect of the league above all else. In the words of one of the founders, Val Edwards (1986), "It is an ideal way to get to know [other lesbians], get out in the sun and have a good time." On the issue of fun, another collective member explained that although there was some ongoing tension between the more competitive and less competitive players, there was always room to be "crazy and silly."

Players routinely engaged in playful banter and antics—for example, hugs all round when outfielders collided while trying to catch a fly ball; and the pitcher hitching up her imaginary jockstrap before the crucial pitch. Open displays of affection between lovers were very common, as well as the usual hugs between friends. Team names like Blue Gays and Lavender Sox attested to the spirit of fun and irony, while the overtly sexual names like Lickety Splits, Juicyfruits and Dykes on Spykes posed clear challenges to compulsory heterosexuality. Not too surprisingly, many women chose not to wear their team shirts on public transportation to and from the game.

On the social side, the Notso collective organized dances, barbecues and bar nights, and players routinely relaxed at a women's bar or club on Sunday afternoons after the game—all time-honoured traditions in lesbian softball dating back at least 20 years (Zipter, 1988). It could be argued that softball is simply the vehicle for the social interaction, as well as the probable sexual activity, that followed the game. Given the scarcity of venues for lesbians to meet one another (when compared to the extensive network of formal and informal avenues for heterosexual liaisons), softball has gained popularity in many lesbian communities because of the friendship and fun it offers, even for women whose athletic skills and backgrounds are limited. And, because the Notsos have been playing every Sunday afternoon throughout the summer since 1984, lesbian softball has become a community social event for players and non-players alike.

Some Visual Images

A brief examination of the images in the 1992–93 Notsos Amazons' calendar will provide some evidence of the ways in which one group of lesbians celebrate physicality and sexuality through sport. These images could be deconstructed much more critically, but I would argue that in analyzing images in a calendar produced by and for lesbians, it is important to apply criteria that recognize this distinctive lesbian context.

For example, some feminists would object to a photo that is cropped to show only a part of a woman's body, if it appeared in a mainstream publication. However, it is possible to view the woman's muscular forearm (September) and leg (July) as a celebration of women's strength and beauty. The same is true of the graceful pitcher (November). In these images, the rolled-up shirt sleeves and the ripped jeans can also be interpreted as lesbian sexual codes. Certainly, the July caption's reference to the whole new meaning of fresh air and red cheeks leaves no doubt about the sexual content. Similarly, the photo of the umpire (February) is accompanied by the umpire's reported comment, "It's been a pleasure perusing your strike zone." I

SEPTEMBER

Notso Amazons' 1992–93
Calendar. Photo by R. Hasner.

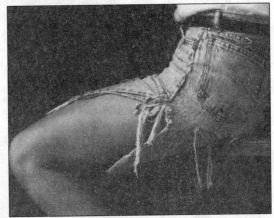

JULY

Notso Amazons' 1992–93
Calendar. Photo by R. Hasner.

NOVEMBER

Notso Amazons' 1992–93
Calendar. Photo by R. Hasner.

FEBRUARY

Notso Amazons' 1992–93
Calendar. Photo by R. Hasner.

MARCH

Notso Amazons' 1992–93
Calendar. Photo by R. Hasner.

APRIL

Notso Amazons' 1992–93
Calendar. Photo by R. Hasner.

JUNE

Notso Amazons' 1992–93
Calendar. Photo by R. Hasner.

would argue that these images represent the open and non-exploitative celebration of women's bodies, from a lesbian perspective.

The photo of women's legs (March) conveys interesting messages
about lesbian styles, as does the batter in the funny hat (April). As
the March caption states, "It's the only league I know where Doc
Martens are considered athletic footwear." Freedom to indulge in
one's distinctive style, either purely for fun, or because it is a crucial
part of one's identity and self-presentation as lesbian, is central to the
Notso spirit. Any and all dress styles are accepted and celebrated. It
is not required that players wear their team shirts, although all players receive one with registration.

Only one of the calendar photos (June) conveys an intimate relationship between the players. It is possible that women did not wish to
pose in ways that indicated a lesbian relationship because they were
apprehensive about being identified in a publication that was to be
widely distributed through women's bookstores. In fact, only five out
of the twelve photos show women clearly enough to be identified; other
photos show women at a distance, or with their backs to the camera.
Dogs appear in two photos, but children are not obvious, even though
there were usually some children among the spectators. Again, fear of
homophobic repercussions may have been a concern for some women.

The images reflect some diversity in terms of body size, age and ethnicity. The calendar has none of the posed, pin-up girl overtones of its malestream counterparts, and the photos are not limited to women who might be considered conventionally attractive by some external standard. As well as humour and irony, the images also portray athletic competence, skill, grace, speed, exhilaration, concentration and determination.

Conclusion

While it is important to acknowledge that power imbalances and exploitative practices can and do occur in lesbian communities, it has been shown that a lesbian sport league, organized on feminist principles, can provide a physically and sexually liberating experience for many women. Enjoyment and friendship through recreational physical activity are priorities for both lesbian and non-lesbian women. The Notsos, like many other lesbian sports leagues, have explicitly addressed these female values and priorities. Additionally, because it is a league organized by and for lesbians, there is opportunity for open celebration of female physicality and sexuality. The game itself allows two avenues of kinesthetic pleasure. Women may enjoy the physical challenge of the game for themselves, and/or they may enjoy watching other women playing the game. In the culture of lesbian softball, these pleasures have implicit sexual dimensions. Thus, the feminist agenda of transforming sport has been realized in this woman-centred model of recreational softball.

7

No Fear?
Lesbians in Sport and Physical Education

"I would love to be able to come out and have every lesbian in sports come out. I think that if that happened, there would be a lot less of this kind of underhanded and subtle discrimination. But stereotypes are hard to break down. I wouldn't know how you'd even begin to go about it."

—Anonymous lesbian coach cited in Brownworth (1994).

In light of critical sport research of the last three decades in North America, Europe, the United Kingdom and Australia, it can be argued that sport continues, for the most part, to serve as the incubator of hegemonic heterosexual masculinity (Messner and Sabo, 1990), while women in general, and lesbians in particular, remain on the margins. However, thanks to the ongoing efforts of lesbian-positive athletes, activists and scholars, there is some evidence of the growing visibility and recognition of lesbians in sport research and sporting practices.

In the following discussion, I will critically review selected research on lesbians in sport and physical education. This is not intended as a comprehensive coverage of every publication on the issue, but rather an overview of trends in research and literature from the 1970s to the mid-1990s. I will begin by examining how the broader issues of gender and sexuality have been taken up in sport literature, and then turn to work that focuses on lesbians' experiences of homophobia and heterosexism in sport, historically and in recent years. A discussion of physical education will follow, and finally, literature on softball will be reviewed as a case study of a sport that is arguably more successful than most in celebrating a lesbian presence in Canadian and American contexts.

My analysis is based on the assumption that a lesbian identity is a political act, and not simply a personal lifestyle. Celia Kitzinger (1987) provides a compelling argument against the privatized, liberal humanist view of sexual "preference" or "lifestyle" as a characteristic that renders the lesbian only minimally different from her heterosexual counterpart. Instead, Kitzinger defines a lesbian in terms of her self-identification, her sociopolitical location and her self-representation as a challenge to the patriarchy. Since liberal humanist views effectively depoliticize lesbian identities, they are not particularly useful to an analysis of the sexual politics of sport. However, this is not to suggest that liberal feminist strategies based on human rights rationales—for example, the inclusion of sexual orientation in harassment policies—do not have a place in the struggle to end homophobia and heterosexism. At the same time, I agree with Kitzinger that the courageous political act of identifying as a lesbian also deserves a positive, proactive response. In sport, this would mean that the lesbian presence is celebrated, and not simply tolerated.

Gender and Sexuality in Sport Research

The 1960s and 1970s marked the beginnings of sport research that took gender and sexuality into account. Metheny's (1965) sport typology presented some implicit messages about sexuality. For example, to engage in sports that involved heavy objects or body contact was to cross over the boundaries of middle-class white "femininity" (and hence to raise the spectre of lesbianism). In a similar vein, sport scholars of the 1970s identified the "apologetic" in women's sport—that is, the practice of paying attention to gender-appropriate modes of self-presentation in dress, hairstyles and general deportment (Felshin, 1973). This was largely in response to the public and media obsession with female athletes' "femininity," as well as sport psychologists' preoccupation with the presumed "role conflict" that these women must experience because of the alleged incompatibility between "femininity" and athletic competence (for critiques, see Allison, 1991; Hall, 1981). Because their sporting activities were perceived as intrusions into the realm of masculinity, sportswomen's sexual identities came under suspicion. According to this line of argument, since sport "made boys into men," it must have a masculinizing effect on women. By this time, it was clear to many, but articulated by few, that *feminine* was a code word for heterosexual.

Sex-role researchers intent on proving that sportswomen, particularly those in traditionally male sports, ranked low on femininity scales, or high on masculinity and androgyny scales, persisted in their efforts as late as 1990 (e.g., Pedersen and Kono, 1990), thus entrenching the very stereotypes that feminists were attempting to dispel. As well as being heterosexist, this line of thinking suggests some confusion between the concepts of sex differentiation, sex-role orientation and sexual orientation. Sex differentiation is based on genetic, morphological, hormonal and social criteria; there is no necessary correlation between morphological or hormonal factors and sexual orientation, and research on the possible genetic roots of sexual orientation remains inconclusive. Sex differentiation based on social criteria is by definition imprecise, since social definitions of sex-appropriate behaviour are subject to specific historical and social-cultural influences.

It is therefore an erroneous and circular argument to claim that heterosexual women are more feminine in their sex-role orientation than lesbians, since culturally specific (North American) definitions of "femininity" are largely based on the appearance and behaviour of heterosexual women, and connotations of "femininity" are closely linked to notions of heterosexual identity and attractiveness. An individual's conformity or nonconformity to prevailing definitions of appropriate sex-role behaviour is a poor predictor of sexual orientation. In the sport context, this means that a woman's self-presentation and playing style in softball, for example, might be perceived as rendering her less "feminine" than her counterpart in figure skating, but such superficial perceptions reveal little about sexual orientation, and much about the social construction of the "feminine" woman and the value placed on the appearance of heterosexual femininity in female sport.

Breaking the Silence

By the 1980s and early 1990s, the advocacy efforts of the women's movements and the lesbian/gay rights movements were having some positive impact on lesbians in sport. Recognition that lesbians do play sport and that homophobia is a pervasive problem was evident in some mainstream sport studies literature. Major physical education and sport studies conferences were beginning to include presentations on homophobia, and the fact that these issues continued to appear on conference programs was a positive sign (e.g., Griffin, 1984; Krane, 1994, 1995; Krane and Pope, 1996; Lenskyj, 1989, 1992b; Sabo, 1987). At the time of writing, however, there is no scholarly anthology focusing exclusively on lesbians in sport, and the *Women in Sport and Physical Activity Journal* was the first to devote a special issue to the topic. A few papers on lesbians' sporting experiences have been presented at conferences or published in sport sociology journals (e.g., Bouchier, 1997; Burroughs, Ashburn and Seebohm, 1995; Fusco, 1992; Krane, 1996; Palzkill, 1990).

Following my own presentation on homophobia in women's sport to the 1989 conference of the North American Society for the Sociology of Sport (Lenskyj, 1989), many women privately shared their own experiences and expressed appreciation that I was working in this area, but these mainstream conferences were not yet experienced as a safe forum for more open discussions of lesbian issues. Even women's sport conferences and organizations were not markedly different. Throughout the 1980s, the liberal position ("we're all the same, let's not talk about differences") prevailed in many women's sport circles.

It is encouraging to note that in the past decade feminist sport researchers have begun to examine the ways in which female sexualities are constructed and constrained by homophobia and heterosexism. Examples include discussions of homophobic attitudes and practices in Canadian women's ice hockey (Etue and Williams, 1996), in U.K. secondary school physical education (Scraton, 1992), and in representations of sexuality in female sport (Hargreaves, 1994; Kane and Greendorfer, 1994). Studies such as these have documented how girls and women in sport experience pressure from family, peers, coaches and the media to present themselves as heterosexual in appearance and behaviour, while at the same time lesbians who prefer to be open about their sexual identities are silenced. The "divide and rule" tactics of homophobic sport leaders and the media effectively deepen the rifts between lesbian and non-lesbian athletes, and, lacking political solidarity, sportswomen have little hope of challenging the male monopoly on sport resources.

In some of this research, the tendency to adopt a liberal humanist perspective remains in evidence. Jennifer Hargreaves, for example, portrays lesbians in the Gay Games as "transcend[ing] the contradictions they face because of their sexuality with their love of sport and the positive focus sport gives to their lives. In this respect their only difference from heterosexual women is their preference for women rather than men as sexual partners" (Hargreaves, 1994; 264). This generalization depoliticizes lesbian identity by reducing it to a sexual preference, and Hargreaves misses the opportunity to examine the place of lesbians in mainstream sport and the place of sport in lesbian subcultures.

Focus on Lesbians in Sport

One of the most significant histories of sexuality and sport in the United States is Susan Cahn's *Coming On Strong* (1994). Her interviews with women growing up and coming out as lesbian in the 1930s, 1940s and 1950s and her analysis of the impact of conservative popular opinion on female physical education and sport provide a comprehensive picture of the uneasy relationship between lesbians and sport. My own work *Out of Bounds: Women, Sport and Sexuality* (1986) examined trends in physical education, the medical establishment and the media from 1890 to the 1980s, with a particular focus on Canada.

On the one hand, women's sport provided a haven for women who preferred a homosocial environment, ostensibly free from pressure to behave and present oneself in a conventionally heterosexual manner, and as such it was well known by lesbians as a place where one might find other lesbians. On the other hand, with growing public, media and commercial interest in women's sport, the "femininity" of all female athletes came under scrutiny and the economic survival of female sport came to rely in large part on an appropriately feminine image (see Chapter 3).

In the Popular Press: *Sports Dykes*

A collection of short stories and essays edited by Susan Fox Rogers titled *Sport Dykes* was published in 1994. While this was not intended as an anthology of research on lesbian athletes, it is nevertheless a valuable addition to the field, and fills a void in both sport fiction and lesbian literature (see Sandoz, 1995).

The essays in *Sport Dykes* provide many important insights into the problem of homophobia, one of the most compelling being Mariah Burton Nelson's account of her experiences coming out as a lesbian in women's professional basketball. Nelson explains how, in the 1980s, an earlier version of this article had been purchased twice—by *Ms.* magazine and *Women's Sports*—but had never appeared in print because of publishers' fears that advertisers would withdraw their accounts from a magazine that mentioned lesbians (Nelson, 1994). This anecdote amply illustrates the obstacles to lesbian visibility in this period, when one of the few sportswomen who was prepared to risk disclosing her lesbian identity was denied the right to do so by publishers concerned about losing advertising dollars. It should be noted that the new *Ms.* magazine which began publication in 1990 has no advertising, precisely because of the fact that advertisers can virtually dictate editorial policy.

Nelson also grapples with the contradictions in lesbian professional athletes' lives in her earlier publication, *Are We Winning Yet?* (1991). Her interviews with lesbian LPGA players revealed how fears of losing sponsorship dollars and popularity with their heterosexual audience resulted in their resentment of openly lesbian fans, and secrecy and shame about their own lesbian identities.

While it is tempting to conclude that economics are the key force behind lesbian in/visibility, other essays in *Sport Dykes* reveal that the issue is more complex. In Brownworth's article on "the competitive closet," a college coach who identified herself as lesbian (but only in her "private life") was among the most homophobic of the women interviewed. Apparently believing the "mannish lesbian" or the "third sex" myth, this coach stated that "people feel they [lesbian players] have an unfair advantage in terms of their physical abilities and they think they intimidate other players ... too many lesbians in women's sports make for a lot of problems that create bad teams and bad team playing and have an overall detrimental effect on the sports themselves" (Brownworth, 1994; 82–83).

I have cited her statement in full in order to point to the barriers to social change in female sport, and the inadequacies of the lesbian/heterosexual dichotomy in understanding the dynamics of homophobia. Although she is lesbian herself, this coach's statement reveals internalized homophobia, not only in her self-hatred, self-denial, and the splitting of her private and public lives, but also in her resentment and hostility towards other lesbians, especially those who are open about their sexuality.

Until the sport climate is more lesbian-positive, it is understandable that some lesbians will develop coping strategies (such as staying "in the closet") that may work in the short term, but in the long term are detrimental both to themselves and to female sport. This vicious circle needs to be interrupted on a number of levels, both individual and institutional, before social change can be effected, and coalitions of lesbian and heterosexual women in sport are needed to add strength and numbers to these interventions. For example, harassment policies should specifically include homophobic harassment; employment policies should identify sexual orientation as prohibited grounds for discrimination in hiring and promotion; health benefits plans should include same-sex partners. It should be routine for same-sex as well as opposite-sex partners to attend sport-related social gatherings, and representations of lesbians should be included in promotional materials such as sport posters and videos—to name just a few everyday acts that would make sport a more welcoming place for lesbians.

Physical Education

Pressure to conceal one's lesbian identity is particularly acute for women who work in physical education (P.E.) with children. The homophobic view that lesbians and gay men are pedophiles still holds sway despite ample evidence to the contrary. Lesbians in post-secondary physical education or athletics face some of the same pressures because of the educational context of their work with adolescents and young adults. Joan Gondola and Toni Fitzpatrick (1985) and Pat Griffin (1989) are among the early physical educators who brought these issues to light. Some 1990s publications focused on lesbians and gay men in education, and some of these examine the specific challenges confronting lesbian P.E. teachers (Clarke, 1993; Harbeck, 1992; Khayatt, 1992; Woods and Harbeck, 1992). Like other lesbians in sport, many lesbian P.E. teachers feared homophobic harassment or loss of their jobs, if they disclosed their sexuality, and so they used the strategy of "passing" as heterosexual, distancing themselves from students and colleagues and from political issues relating to homosexuality and lesbianism. At the same time, others enjoyed the less formal dress code in P.E. that made the act of "passing" somewhat easier. Despite school environments "deeply enveloped in homophobia and heterosexism," a minority of teachers actively confronted the issues and supported lesbian and gay students (Woods and Harbeck, 1992; 160).

As Sherry Woods and Karen Harbeck persuasively argue, because homophobia and heterosexism have a negative impact not only on lesbians but on all physical educators, male and female, heterosexual and homosexual, collective action on the part of the entire profession is necessary to deal with the fear and isolation experienced by lesbian and gay colleagues. It is therefore encouraging to see that some Canadian and American P.E. organizations led the way in putting homophobia on their conference agendas (Sabo, 1987; Griffin, 1989; Griffin and Genasci, 1990). However, as Nancy Bouchier (1997) has documented in her analysis of lesbian sport history, there is still significant opposition to open discussion of these issues in some P.E. circles.

Outside Sport Studies

Discussions of issues facing lesbians in sport have occasionally appeared in women's studies and lesbian/gay studies literature, and, more recently, in queer studies and cultural studies. Examples include a chapter in one of the earliest lesbian studies anthologies, edited by

Margaret Cruikshank in 1982, on lesbians in a university physical education department (Cobhan, 1982), and an autobiographical piece by a retired professional tennis player that appeared in Marcy Adelman's 1986 anthology on older lesbians (Anonymous, 1986). It is significant that neither author used her real name, and that both cited the need to protect the identities of other women with whom they were associated. In the current political climate, it is now possible for many (but certainly not all) lesbians to identify themselves when writing about these issues.

In cultural studies, examples include analyses of heterosexual image-making in figure skating, exemplified by the infamous "good girl/bad girl" Kerrigan/Harding controversy in the 1995 anthology *Women on Ice* (Baughman, 1995), and a discussion of Martina Navratilova and "popular culture's romance with lesbianism" in the 1994 collection *The Good, the Bad and the Gorgeous* (Hamer and Budge, 1994). As Diane Hamer (1994; 77) explains, Navratilova has come to represent a target of desire for two audiences, representing, for heterosexuals, "the horror and fascination of deviance" and, for lesbians, a celebration of our sexual identity.

A number of theorists influenced by postmodernism and feminism, including Susan Bordo and Liz Grosz, discuss the related issues of the female body, physicality and sexuality (Bordo, 1989; Grosz, 1987) and their work is often cited by critical sport scholars in examinations of the social construction of the female sporting body (e.g., Cole, 1993; Hall, 1993, 1996). From another perspective, Holly Devor's 1989 study of women who "pass" as men, and Phyllis Burke's 1996 exposé of psychiatrists' creation of Gender Identity Disorder, both draw important links between sporting interests and the social construction of heterosexual femininity, confirming yet again the dominant view of sport as masculine and/or masculinizing.

Out to the Ball Game

In any discussion of lesbians in sport, the game of softball deserves its own category. Journalist Yvonne Zipter was one of the first to produce a popular book on the topic, *Diamonds Are a Dyke's Best Friend* (1988), which presents important documentation and discussion of the history and current status of lesbian softball, with a clear political perspective. Softball has long represented a safe alternative to bars as a place to meet and socialize with other lesbians. In the past two decades, the development of lesbian leagues in many major Canadian and American cities has continued this tradition, but with added political impact because of their open identification as a lesbian (or lesbian-positive) space. Moreover, leagues which are organized along feminist principles of inclusiveness regarding sporting skills and physical ability, as well as ethnicities and socioeconomic status, constitute a significant challenge to mainstream female sport (Birrell and Richter, 1987).

The All American Girls' Baseball League of the 1940s and 1950s gained a high profile with the 1992 release of the film *A League of Their Own*. (Many references to women's baseball actually refer to softball, which remains the more common female sport, but in the case of the All Americans, these women did in fact play baseball.) Not too surprisingly, the film did not do justice to the strong lesbian presence in the league, although its treatment of the mandatory Charm School did provide some implicit critique of the management's preoccupation with "femininity." (One wonders whether a mainstream film on the LPGA or women's NCAA today would be equally critical of the "image consultants" hired by these homophobic institutions to help players present a conventionally heterosexual image.)

Lois Browne's 1992 book, *Girls of Summer*, provides a critique of the double standard that required players to "look like girls" and "play like men." Browne documents how league organizers were preoccupied with eliminating any "outward signs" of lesbianism—short hair and sensible footwear, for example (Browne, 1992; Johnson, 1994; Ferrante, 1996). As is the case with other female sports that attract public and media attention, keeping up (heterosexual) appearances was high on organizers' list of priorities.

Susan Johnson's (1994) oral and documentary history *When Women Played Hardball* clearly identifies the classism and homophobia at work in the league's codes of behaviour and dress, as well as the overt racism in their selection procedures. However, Johnson presents a fairly sympathetic view of the way in which players and managers recognized and respected the private lives of the significant numbers who were lesbian. She emphasizes that, in an era where young working-class women had limited information about sexuality and were discouraged from discussing sexual issues at all, this silence surrounding lesbianism did not necessarily signify the level of homophobia that it might today. In a similar vein, Susan Cahn (1994) discusses the "play it, don't say it" code of behaviour followed by many lesbian athletes of that era, and explains how they conveyed their presence "primarily through action, style and unspoken understandings" (187) while taking care not to cross the line in the "mannish" behaviour banned by league organizers. However, "play it, don't say it" sounds disturbingly similar to "don't ask, don't tell," and whether it be in the 1940s or in the 21st century, such codes of silence are ultimately destructive.

Even the 1995 Canadian National Film Board production titled *Baseball Girls*, which documents historical and contemporary developments in the sport, reflects the "play it, don't say it" code. Not only is there no spoken recognition that baseball is a sport practised by women of all sexualities (although this may have been obvious to viewers attuned to lesbian codes of self-presentation), but excessive attention was paid the heterosexuality of (some of) the women portrayed. Largely irrelevant topics such as players' images of the "ideal man," their marriage plans, and their sexual interest in the male umpire were given unnecessary airtime, in the filmmakers' apparent attempt to establish the heterosexual credentials of all involved (Siegel, 1995). Market forces cannot be blamed entirely for this emphasis, since the National Film Board is subsidized by the federal government and has in the past produced films that authentically portrayed women of all sexual preferences (e.g., an openly lesbian, hearing-impaired woman in *Beyond Intimacy*, a film on women with disabilities). One can only conclude that the world of sport was considered, perhaps correctly, too homophobic to permit lesbian softball players to come out on film.

Conclusion

Although there is evidence that the links between gender, sexuality and sport are increasingly being addressed in the critical sport literature, relatively little has been written about lesbians' actual experiences, positive or negative, in sport. Invisibility remains a key force fuelling discrimination against lesbians in sport in the 1990s. For lesbians on sport's front lines, like the Olympic coach cited at the beginning of this article, the barriers posed by heterosexism and homophobia seem insurmountable. These women rightly fear harassment, violence, ostracism and job loss if their identities become known; as well, they are likely to be blamed for giving women's sport "a bad name" and driving away potential sponsors and allies.

Those of us who work in the somewhat more liberal realm of university-based sport studies may be better positioned to influence policy making and bring about social change—if not in attitudes, at least in behaviour—in order to warm up the chilly climate for lesbians in sport. By naming homophobia as one of the most pervasive social problems in female sport, and by actively celebrating the lesbian presence in sport, sport scholars can make a positive step towards breaking the silence and ending the invisibility.

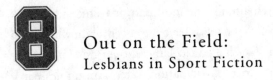

Out on the Field:
Lesbians in Sport Fiction

"I know coaches and what they're like ... You have to look beyond that and find a balance between ego and reality. Right now all you are is a female version of a male jock, strutting around lapping up the adulation and screwing any woman who gets within half a mile."

—Sharika to her girlfriend Casey,
in Kristen Garrett's *Lady Lobo* (1993; 117).

Women's long-standing marginalization in sport, achieved either through explicit exclusionary policies or implicit anti-woman attitudes and practices, is reflected in the paucity of sport novels written by women and/or having women as central characters. Moreover, the few novels that are woman-centred rarely include openly lesbian characters. Therefore, the following analysis of women's sport fiction will focus on portrayals of lesbian athletes.

Lesbian Invisibility

There is relatively little documentation of lesbians' sporting experiences, largely because, in the male-dominated world of sport, it has been unsafe for lesbians to disclose their sexual identities or share their experiences. Thus, lesbians remain, for the most part, invisible in women's sport history, and only since the 1980s have they been acknowledged in sport sociology research. This is a particularly serious omission in view of the relatively high sport participation rates among lesbians. Considerable evidence points to the fact that lesbians are overrepresented in the ranks of sportswomen, and various explanations have been offered. It has been suggested, for example, that women who are nonconforming in terms of sexuality may also choose to be nonconforming in terms of recreational activities, and that women-only sport provides a relatively safe social context for women to meet other women (Nelson, 1991; Palzkill, 1990; Zipter, 1988).

Reflecting some of the major trends in Canada, the United States and the United Kingdom since the beginning of the 20th century, fictional representations of lesbian athletes, albeit limited in number, add an important dimension to lesbians' sport history. Many fictional portrayals of lesbians' sport experiences bear close correspondence to the few biographical sources that do exist (e.g., Adelman, 1986; Rogers, 1994), a pattern which suggests that the authors were drawing on personal experiences.

I begin with the assumption that lesbian sport fiction both describes and helps to constitute readers' attitudes to sport, and in so doing provides avenues for both accommodation and resistance to hegemonic femininity. The theoretical assumptions underlying this analysis are derived from feminist analyses of sexism and homophobia (Pharr, 1988) and from the neo-marxist concepts of hegemony, emphasized femininity, accommodation and resistance (Connell, 1987). The notion of lesbian in/visibility will be used to explicate the complex survival strategies adopted by lesbians in the hostile climate of mainstream sport.

Women, Sport and Sexuality: Historical Attitudes

In Canada, the United States and the U.K., sportswomen have long been viewed as transgressing the boundaries of appropriate feminine behaviour. Such transgressions often provoked public scrutiny of sportswomen's sexuality since it was assumed that their desire to "intrude" into the male realm of sport indicated some sexual abnormality—for example, that they wanted to be men or that they were lesbian. Clearly, the stereotype of the "mannish lesbian athlete" shaped this kind of thinking. Guardians of hegemonic femininity—educators, doctors, journalists and others—issued warnings about the masculinizing effects of sport on girls and women. Throughout the first half of the 20th century, women's sport was seen as the domain of women who, either by example or by active recruitment, posed a threat to "normal" girls and women (Cahn, 1994; Lenskyj, 1986).

In the early decades of the century, with increasing medical interest in the field of sexology, there was growing public awareness that lesbians did exist, and that they posed a threat to traditional power relations between the sexes (Faderman, 1981, 1991). At a time when middle-class women were entering higher education in unprecedented numbers, and schools and universities were establishing organized sporting programs for both sexes, women were perceived as breaking too many traditional barriers. In the U.S., in particular, critics of higher education, joining in the prevailing discourse on "race suicide," pointed to the lower marriage and motherhood rates of college graduates. At the same time, critics of female sport emphasized the strain to reproductive functioning posed by vigorous activity and the emotional stress of sporting competition. In relation to both higher education and sport, authorities expressed concern about the intimate female friendships fostered in these homosocial settings. Up to this time, there had been more concern about the negative effects of the "mingling of the sexes" in educational and sport contexts, and the need for chaperones for female teams, than about the alleged problem of same-sex friendships.

Women's schools and colleges provided middle-class girls and women with a variety of opportunities for sport and physical activity. Questions were rarely raised about the physical culture program, which was legitimized by elaborate "scientific" rationales. Individualized gymnastic programs, performed under the instructor's watchful eye, would improve young women's health, posture, "functional health" and motherhood potential (Inness, 1993; Somers, 1930). In contrast, team sports and interscholastic competition were identified as threats to femininity and motherhood, and by the 1930s, many of these activities had been diluted or eliminated. With them went the opportunity for young women to escape some of the constraints of hegemonic femininity and heterosexuality.

In the Beginning: *The Well of Loneliness*

Although it cannot be classified as sport fiction, Radycliffe Hall's pioneering lesbian novel, *The Well of Loneliness*, first published 1928, provides a classic example of a fictional lesbian whose preferred activities included "masculine" sports (Hall, 1968). Stephen Gordon, the main character, epitomizes what lesbian theorist Esther Newton has termed "the mythic mannish lesbian" (Newton, 1984). In an apparent attempt to develop a consistent lesbian characterization, Hall and others of this genre and era gave stereotypically masculine attributes to many of their lesbian characters. This so-called "natural" tendency towards masculinity is apparently intended by way of explanation for the character's lesbian identity—she should have been born male, so the argument goes.

As a girl, Stephen is portrayed as strong and muscular, more adept at playing cricket and climbing trees than some of her male peers. She is contemptuous of girls of her age who have been raised to be fragile and delicate, and dislikes traditional girls' play activities. Even at a young age, Stephen accompanies her father on horseback on the fox hunt, and is an accomplished rider. Her father teaches her to ride astride, at a time when middle-class propriety demanded that girls and women ride sidesaddle. Hall's early portrayal of a lesbian character who rejects activities and attributes associated with femininity, and prefers to develop her masculine athletic talents and interests, foreshadowed many later lesbian characters in both sport fiction and lesbian literature.

Sport Fiction, College Fiction and Schoolgirl Stories

Like other print media, sport fiction can be seen as both dramatizing and reinforcing social relations of everyday life. For women—especially for lesbians—novels offered an avenue of resistance—an opportunity to celebrate women's intimate friendships and women's sport at a time when both were under attack. Sherrie Inness (1993, 1994) has documented the ways in which girls' college fiction in the U.S. from the 1890s to the 1930s served to socialize young female readers in apparently contradictory ways. It validated intimate female friendships (known in this period as "crushes") and promoted shared community values in the homosocial world of the women's college, while, at the same time, it prepared young women for their future roles as middle-class wives and mothers. Hence, its potentially counter-hegemonic agenda was considerably weakened by the traditional messages about women's destiny.

Examining college sport specifically, Inness noted that American college stories for girls routinely included a chapter or short story about athletic women, and she convincingly demonstrated how the sporting content constituted "fictional resistance" to the individualistic physical culture agenda of this period (1993; 106–107). Similarly, in the "schoolgirl stories" of British novelists such as Elsie Oxenham and Angela Brazil, sport is a common motif. Team sports and country dancing were mandatory in English private girls' schools and central to the plot of many of these novels (Auchmuty, 1989). On both sides of the Atlantic, schoolgirl stories and college fiction often portrayed sporting competition as the stage on which interpersonal as well as team and school loyalties were played out. Intimate friendships between young women were presented openly and unapologetically, as indeed they existed in everyday life. Visual images of sportswomen from this period similarly reveal these women's spontaneous physical intimacy and the spirit of playfulness (Nelson, 1991).

In her review of British "schoolgirl stories" from the 1920s on, Rosemary Auchmuty (1989) claims that, as the century progressed, writers fell victim to the growing public censure of close female friendships, prompted by sexologists' warnings of "abnormal" sexual development. Whereas in the earlier novels, intimate and passionate relationships between the young women were validated, and husbands were presented as an impediment, the later novels empha-sized heterosexual romance, marriage and motherhood. This is not to suggest that close female relationships did not continue after the 1920s, but rather that they were no longer viewed as appropriate subjects for juvenile fiction (Simmons, 1979). American college fiction displayed the effects of this censure several decades earlier, with the pathologizing of intimate female friendships occurring as early as 1915 (Inness, 1994).

In 1946, Josephine Tey, a British mystery writer, published *Miss Pym Disposes*. Set in England in the 1940s, the novel focuses on the Leys Physical Training College, a women-only college for physical education teachers and a hotbed of intimate female friendships, where "crushes" between the young women (or between the young women and their older instructors) are virtually taken for granted. With two exceptions, none of the numerous female characters expresses any romantic interest in men. This was an unusual pattern for a novel appearing as late as 1946, since by this time most college fiction was emphasizing heterosexual romance. (It is possible, however, that because the novel's sport content comprised only dance and gymnastics, and not more radical activities such as competitive team sports, potential critics were mollified.)

In *Miss Pym Disposes*, the action centres on senior students in their demanding final term at the physical education college, culminating in a public exhibition of dance and gymnastics. Tey develops a picture of attractive young women in the prime of youth, glowing with health and energy. Even though the rigours of study and gymnastic practice have taken their toll on the students, Miss Pym never ceases to admire their physical attractiveness. It is clear that Miss Pym (and perhaps Miss Tey herself) finds the situation exciting and engaging. There is no attempt to undermine the young women's joyous physicality, open affection and spirit of playfulness.

Only one character, a Brazilian student who is new to the British boarding school, is openly critical of the relationship between Pamela Nash (nicknamed Beau, and presumably, the more "mannish" partner) and Mary Innes, key players in the subsequent murder. The two young women are openly affectionate and make no attempt to hide their relationship, although it is not explicitly portrayed as sexual. Beau spends holidays with Mary's family, who welcome and admire her. However, Tey resorts to the melodramatic device of dissolving the lesbian relationship through a tragedy, thereby conforming to the common pattern of "tragic endings" in lesbian novels of this era (Foster, 1985).

Almost Invisible: Lesbians in Sport Fiction in the 1970s and 1980s

In the 1980s, public disclosures by prominent athletes such as Martina Navratilova and Dave Kopay have raised awareness of the presence of lesbians and gay men in sport. However, lesbians are still, for the most part, invisible in women's sport, as well as in sport fiction by and about women. Sport literature of the 1970s and 1980s does not fully reflect the dramatic increases in female sporting participation in those decades, or the growing strength of the women's and lesbian and gay rights movements. From the 1970s on, there have been very few novels with sportswomen—lesbian or heterosexual—as the main characters. What follows is a critical review of selected sport novels with strong lesbian themes.

In 1978, Marge Piercy, a well-known feminist novelist, published *The High Cost of Living*, a book that provides an interesting commentary on sexual politics in urban America in the 1970s. The main character is Leslie, a 23-year-old lesbian living in a working-class Detroit neighbourhood. She is a graduate student in history, who by the end of the novel has achieved a black belt in karate. Her interest in karate is a central theme, and in the end it serves as a means of putting her relatively liberal feminist leanings into action.

Leslie had been the victim of a man's homophobic attack and realizes that she had no idea how to fight back. Karate, for her, is a means of bodily empowerment, a physical activity that she does for herself, and she finds the techniques pleasurable. She is proud of her muscles, because "every muscle represents years of effort" (103). During a period of extreme loneliness, she had felt ugly, but when she caught sight of herself in a mirror while practising karate, she was once more reassured that her body was strong and graceful—it was good "the way a good race horse was good" (193).

In her evolving friendship with Honor, a 17-year-old high school student, Leslie tries to share her view of her body as an asset rather than a liability. Trying to discourage Honor's preoccupation with fashion and makeup, she explains, "The way I look, that's how I look when I wake up, when I get out of the shower, when I make love. It's just me, all the way through" (103).

One of Leslie's faithful friends, Tasha, is a committed feminist activist with a special interest in a collectively operated Women's

School. Initially, Leslie is contemptuous of the idea, and rejects
Tasha's invitation to teach a history course, labelling women's history
"old wives' tales" (197). However, after she achieves her black belt,
she decides to volunteer to teach a women's self-defence course at the
school. At the same time, she continues to struggle with her conflict
over immersing herself in the lesbian political community or competing for the scarce rewards of the mainstream world. At the end of her
first self-defence class, deeply moved by the needs of these women
and their obvious alienation from their bodies, she makes a symbolic
gesture of reconciling her two worlds by having the women join
hands and form a circle.

Piercy's novel, like some more recent sport fiction, uses a sporting
activity as the protagonist's route to a deeper feminist consciousness
and a stronger commitment to feminist activism. While this is a valid
and commendable theme, the common fictional juxtaposition of the
two characters—the non-athletic, political feminist and the pre-polit-
ical or apolitical sportswoman—reinforces damaging stereotypes and
does a disservice to those athletes who have, in fact, been politically
active in women's sport and other feminist issues since the 1970s.

American novelist R.R. Knudson deserves to be mentioned here,
although none of her characters is explicitly lesbian. The main character in her juvenile fiction (e.g., 1972, 1975, 1977, 1978, 1984) is Zan
Hagen, a gifted all-round high school athlete. Zan's (unofficial) coach
and best friend (but not boyfriend) is a completely unathletic boy
called Arthur Rinehart. Like many female characters in sport fiction,
Zan is single-minded in her pursuit of success in the male-defined
world of sport, and as one commentary noted, Knudson allows Zan
"the same sort of impossible athletic triumphs fictional boys had been
enjoying for decades" (Oriard, 1986; 5).

However, Zan is scathing in her assessment of girls who have no
interest in the rough and tumble of sport, and the characterization
of the overweight female coach as a "giant, red-faced dimwit"

(Knudson, 1977; 22) borders on cruelty. Knudson juxtaposes the philosophy of the female physical education teacher, who is more intent on promoting "ladylike" play than athletic skills, with Zan's and Rinehart's emphasis on "serious" training, aggressive play and winning at all costs. Zan has no romantic interest in boys, but in most of the novels she has few close female friends, either. Presumably her dedication to winning and her relationship with Rinehart fill all her social and emotional needs.

Knudson has been justly criticized for her books' liberal agenda (Griffin, 1985). The overall message is that women must act like men, play men's sport, and gain male approval in order to be taken seriously. The male world of sport remains unchanged, and only a few exceptional girls and women can enter it. Perhaps in a later era, with the gains made by the women's movement and lesbian and gay activism, Knudson would have had greater freedom to develop openly lesbian characters and alternative sporting models.

Rita Mae Brown is a novelist whose works include a number of "sex-variant" characters, including lesbians, gays, transvestites and transsexuals. In *Sudden Death* (1983), Carmen is a 24-year-old professional tennis player from Argentina, now living in the U.S. She is in a lesbian relationship with Harriet, a university professor now in the role of "tennis wife," financially supported by Carmen's substantial winnings. However, given the homophobia of the tennis circuit, lesbian players and their partners are firmly closeted. Carmen is portrayed as a totally self-absorbed and overindulged "love-junkie," incapable of understanding why Harriet would want to work at such a low-paying job. "She could understand a baseball player's life, but not a professor's" (28). Again, we see the characterization of the mindless lesbian "jock" and her more cerebral, politicized partner. The fact that Brown herself had an affair with a famous tennis player (Martina Navratilova) has been mentioned by critics of this book as an explanation for Carmen's negative portrayal.

In Brown's novel, a media scandal about Carmen's lesbian relationship prompts Harriet to tell reporters that she is gay. She takes the position that she has to be honest, whereas Carmen's willingness to lie is portrayed as purely financial self-interest. Brown's fictional treatment of lesbian in/visibility on the women's tennis circuit in the 1970s and 1980s was confirmed by investigative journalist Michael Mewshaw in the 1990s. His research identified the high level of homophobia in professional tennis, as seen, for example, in public and parental concern that lesbian players might "recruit" young, impressionable adolescents. Mewshaw found that some parents, in fact, approved exploitative relationships between young female players (some as young as 16) and their older male coaches, on the grounds that at least these arrangements protected their daughters from falling prey to the lesbian players (Mewshaw, 1993). On the issue of parental control, Martina Navratilova's mystery novel, *The Total Zone* (Navratilova and Nickles, 1994), provides a graphic and disturbing portrayal of the physical and sexual violence suffered by an adolescent player at the hands of her father/coach.

Sudden Death has been criticized as prose "worthy of the *National Enquirer*" (Oriard, 1986); at the very least, it can be characterized as a polemic. However, despite the nasty characterization of most of the female tennis players, heterosexual or lesbian, the author confronts a number of key issues for lesbians in professional sport. For example, in a debate between women's tennis officials and potential sponsors over players' marketability, the player's talent is less relevant than her heterosexual attractiveness when a company is looking for an appropriate marketing image. Soon after the scandal about Carmen's lesbian relationship, the Women's Tennis Guild initiates a dress code (nail polish, nylons, perfume and skirts). Brown characterizes this official reaction as "tennis's version of the McCarthy period," and it is significant that similar dress codes continue to operate in many women's sports today.

A New Perspective: Lesbian Sport Fiction since the 1980s

The influence of liberal feminism is evident in Jenifer Levin's 1982 novel *Water Dancer*, which poses a challenge to the mainstream "heroic quest" genre of sport fiction. The main lesbian character is Dorey, a young marathon swimmer who is determined to swim the cold and dangerous waters of San Antonio Straits. Rather than viewing herself as a "giant" who dominates the water and her opponents, Dorey has reached the point of surrendering to the water, and now sees herself as a "water dancer."

The characters in this novel—male and female, lesbian and heterosexual—are multidimensional, and thoughtful portrayals, such as Levin's, of a wide spectrum of friendships and relationships are rare in sport fiction. However, apart from Dorey's symbiotic rather than dominant relationship with the water, it is difficult to see how her obsession with marathon swimming and her brutal self-discipline differ significantly from that of any of her male counterparts. Indeed, one analysis of the novel (Carson and Horvath, 1991) claims that Dorey is suffering from gender confusion, ultimately resolved by her rejection of femininity and her adoption of conventional masculine competitive behaviour.

While this is a plausible explanation for Dorey's approach to swimming, it fails to address the explicitly sexual questions raised by Levin. During the course of the novel, Dorey has sexual encounters with her coach, Sarge, and also with his wife, Ilana, who has long played the role of nurturer to the young male swimmers at Sarge's training camp. Examining this aspect of the novel, Christian Messenger (1990; 181) proposes that the two relationships represent the complementary masculine and feminine narratives of discipline and nurture. However, the novel leaves most details of emotional and sexual ties between Dorey and Ilana unexplored, and in the end it is unclear which relationship Dorey is willing to sacrifice. Although the lack of resolution of Dorey's sexual identity is not itself a problem, it is disappointing for readers hoping to find a validating portrayal of a bisexual or lesbian athlete. In fact, one is reminded of Robert Towne's film, *Personal Best*, also produced in the early 1980s, in which a lesbian relationship between two Olympic runners is soon replaced by "the real thing"—heterosexual sex.

Both *Water Dancer* and *Personal Best* have some troubling features. They validate older male coaches' seduction of young female athletes, and they imply that such encounters serve as a corrective for these young women's lesbian tendencies. At the same time, neither author attempts to downplay the coaches' anger at their protegee's sexual activities, and I would expect that a reader/viewer could readily recognize the implicit threat of rape signalled by these outbursts. However, this is clearly not the case. Discussing Sarge's violent response in *Water Dancer*, Messenger (1990; 178) attributes it simply to "male frustration," possessiveness and feelings of "estrangement from the female," rather than reading any threat into the episode. From my subject position as woman and lesbian, I would argue that Levin was attempting, apparently without total success, to portray an extremely threatening situation for both Ilana and Dorey, and not simply a crisis in male identity for Sarge.

Jenifer Levin's latest novel, *The Sea of Light* (1993), reflects a more sophisticated analysis of sport as a context for women's social and sexual relationships. The novel presents three major lesbian characters: Bren, a university swimming coach who is mourning the death of her lover, Kay, an English professor; Babe, a former competitive swimmer of Cuban origin, who is recovering from the physical and mental trauma of surviving an airplane crash; and Ellie, team captain and the daughter of Holocaust survivors. Multiple narrators are used, and each chapter is presented from a different character's perspective.

Bren, the oldest of the lesbian characters, is relatively secure in her sexual identity but determined to keep it a secret. She puts considerable energy into maintaining a professional distance between herself and team members, especially the lesbian swimmers. She is portrayed as a woman with an all-encompassing commitment to competitive swimming, and a reluctance to consider any critiques of competitive sport. Bren is clearly an advocate of the "no pain, no gain" school of coaching. She fits Kay's cynical title of "Super Coach"—with her well-developed sense of the Protestant work ethic, she views winning as just a job. In a stereotypical portrayal of campus politics, it is Kay, the non-athlete, who is interested in women's studies and critical of competitive sport, while all the athletes are too immersed in sporting competition to concern themselves with political issues.

Both Babe and Ellie, young women in their early twenties, are struggling with their sexual identities, but soon confirm their attraction for each other and by the end of the novel are in a long-term relationship. Unlike many lesbian characters in sport novels, these women are not portrayed as physically perfect. Having survived two days of exposure in the Atlantic after the crash, as well as surgery for sport-related injuries, Babe's body is a mass of scars. However, Ellie finds beauty in Babe's strength and muscularity.

Two 1988 novels, Judith Alguire's *All Out* and Joyce Bright's *Sunday's Child*, have women's marathon running as a central theme and both are produced by feminist publishers—Naiad and New Victoria. The main character in *All Out* is Kay Strachan, an internationally successful runner who is a true amateur—she works for a living as a pharmacist rather than accepting commercial endorsements. Although little is made of this, it appears that Kay is of Native Canadian origin. Kay's roommate, best friend and occasional lover is Tab, a university teacher and political lesbian. Like other lesbian athletes in this genre, Kay is an apolitical lesbian dedicated to sporting victory, while her non-athlete partner, Tab, is the often polemic voice of lesbian-feminist analysis of sport and society. An unexpected character is Kay's coach, Bill—a quiet, unemotional Quebecker who displays few of the "no pain, no gain" beliefs evident in most coaches, real or fictitious, male or female.

Tab is portrayed as unsupportive of Kay's training routine and dedication to running, as well as critical of competitive sport on political grounds. "What do sports really do to advance women?" she asks. "They benefit only the elite, those few women at the top, particularly those who fit the male notion of what a female athlete should look like." And she concludes, "Sport fosters competition rather than cooperation. Cooperation is the key to advancement" (15).

Conflict between Kay and Tab is both political and personal, although, in a somewhat unexpected ending, Kay proposes that they attempt a permanent, monogamous relationship. The political gap between the two women is exemplified when Tab pressures Kay to attend her lesbian feminist discussion group to talk about women's sport. One member accuses Kay of "sacrificing the lesbian-feminist movement for a shoe contract." The group subsequently decides to go on record as "opposing competition in sport" (45–46). At a later meeting, the group votes to stage a demonstration against the women's Olympic marathon, the race that promises to be the culmination of Kay's running career.

Early in the novel, Kay is determined to keep her sexual identity secret, but by the end, she is prepared to take a more radical stance. At the award ceremony following her winning marathon run at the Montreal Olympics, she wears a button with the caption "Mother Nature Is a Lesbian." Tab's feelings for Kay are changed dramatically by Kay's brave action, which she interprets as a statement on behalf of all women. However, Kay denies this, and says that she did it for Tab—an individual gesture rather than a political statement. In any event, the theme of Kay's burgeoning feminist consciousness makes this novel similar to the others reviewed here in terms of its stereotypical characters.

In Joyce Bright's novel *Sunday's Child*, Kate, the main character, also has her sights set on the Olympics, and hopes to make a comeback at the age of 38. At the beginning of the novel, Kate is in a heterosexual relationship. Her running partner and closest friend, Angie, is lesbian, and predictably, the two become lovers by the end of the novel. A compelling sub-theme is the mystery of the serial rapist whose targets include lesbians and female runners. Both women are deeply affected by the rapist—Angie as a burnt-out rape crisis counsellor and Kate as a survivor of child sexual abuse. The novel has a clear feminist message in its treatment of sexual violence, women's friendships and female sexualities. Unlike many other lesbian sport novels, it does not set up the lesbian athlete as apathetic to political issues.

Lady Lobo, by Kristen Garrett (1993), represents a new wave of lesbian sport fiction, which might be termed contemporary lesbian "pulp"; Garrett's portrayals of young lesbians' sexual encounters are colourful, to say the least. Published by an explicitly feminist press, the novel presents a realistic view of the brutal world of American college basketball, but with little hint of critique. Although, it could be argued that none is needed, since the novel speaks for itself.

Casey, the main lesbian character, is a young women recruited from high school for a college team. Her two loves are basketball and women, but she avoids serious relationships that might interfere with her basketball career. However, by the end of the novel, Casey's mercurial and mysterious affair with Sharika, an older Black women who is a former professional tennis player, promises to become a long-term relationship. Garrett's treatment of interracial tensions among the players is not particularly insightful, but her attempt to grapple with racism is itself noteworthy for this genre.

The players' love–hate relationship with the coach (a heterosexual woman) is illuminating, as is the coach's use of graduate students as disciplinarians for the team, presumably so that players will displace their anger on their peers and continue to worship and obey the coach. All aspects of players' lives are policed: what they eat and drink, whom they date, whether they meet the curfew. In any other context, such controlling and abusive behaviour directed at young women would be condemned. In women's competitive sport, as this novel portrays, the goal is to win, no matter what the cost.

In view of the central place of softball in lesbian life in Canada and the U.S., this sport has a surprisingly low profile in lesbian sport fiction. Yvonne Zipter's history of lesbian softball, *Diamonds Are a Dyke's Best Friend* (1988), demonstrates how softball has for decades served as an unofficial meeting place for lesbians, both as players and as spectators. It also provides an appropriate context for feminist alternatives to highly competitive sport, as leagues experiment with more woman-friendly rules and organizing structures.

Conclusion

This review demonstrates the relatively untapped potential of sport as a theme in lesbian fiction, and the dearth of lesbian characters in sport fiction and women's fiction. At the same time, there is little doubt that lesbians are overrepresented in the ranks of sportswomen, and that sport has long played an important role in the social life of Canadian and American lesbian communities (Cahn, 1994; Rogers, 1994; Zipter, 1988). Significantly, four of the five female characters examined by Messenger (1990) in his discussion of women in sport narratives were lesbian or bisexual. However, in two instances, the female character's connection to sport was primarily through her relationships with male football players—a disappointing pattern that reflected the paucity of woman-centred sport narratives in 1990.

It is interesting to contrast the slow development of the lesbian sport novel with the rapidly growing (and more cerebral) genre of the lesbian mystery (Breazeale, 1994). In this field, many of the protagonists—police officers, private investigators or self-proclaimed "detectives"—are portrayed as strong, muscular women, in top physical condition, competent in martial arts or outdoor survival skills.

Jeane Harris's Delia Ironfoot and Claire McNab's Carol Ashton are good examples. Lesbian mysteries portray physical competence as a means to an end—a way of ensuring that the hero can extricate herself and her loved ones from dangerous situations, often in the interests of some larger social justice project. In contrast, lesbian sport novels posit winning or achieving a personal best performance as the primary goal, and, among many non-sporting feminists, such a goal can easily be dismissed as trivial.

Feminist sport advocates have for several decades lamented non-sporting feminists' general lack of interest in the politics of women's sport, and it appears that many feminist and lesbian novelists are equally uninterested in the topic. Perhaps, in real life as well as in fiction, the stereotype of female "jocks" as apolitical leads novelists to assume that there is no market for woman-centred sport fiction, or that androcentric sporting practices are too entrenched to allow for woman-centred alternatives.

This is not to discount the small number of authors who are exploring the tensions and contradictions experienced by female athletes, both lesbian and heterosexual. These novelists are now beginning to grapple with the complex social issues of misogyny, homophobia, sexual violence, racism and the "win at all costs" ethos of malestream sport. Although very few manage to avoid the stereotypical juxtaposition of the non-athletic feminist and the non-feminist athlete, most acknowledge, either implicitly or explicitly, that the fact of being lesbian in the sport context—being "out on the field"—is itself a political act.

Gay Games or Gay Olympics?
Implications for Lesbian Inclusion

The Purpose of the Gay Games is "to foster and augment the self-respect of lesbians and gay men ... and to engender respect and understanding from the non-gay world."

—Federation of Gay Games (1997).

When the first Gay Games, at that time called the "Gay Olympic Games," were held in San Francisco in 1982, they were hailed as an empowering sporting and cultural celebration organized by and for lesbians, gays and their allies on the principles of inclusion and participation. (The Gay Games are open to participants who are gay, lesbian, bisexual, transgendered, queer, and heterosexual, but the terms most often used in reference to the Gay Games–related communities are *lesbian and gay*. Since most of the discussion here concerns events of the 1980s and 1990s, the terms lesbian and gay are historically appropriate.)

From their inception, discrimination based on "sexual orientation, gender, race, religion, nationality, ethnic origin, political belief(s), athletic/artistic ability, physical challenge, or HIV status" was prohibited. Since their modest beginnings in a San Francisco football stadium, the Gay Games have grown into an international sporting spectacle and business enterprise, with more than 20 core sporting events, a high level of competition between bidding cities, budgets exceeding US$7 million, corporate sponsors and more participants than most Olympic Games have attracted.

Organizing for Social Change

For many Canadian and American lesbian and gay activists in the early 1980s, an enterprise such as the Gay Games represented a radical departure from their usual political work, in that it was primarily a proactive initiative—a sport and cultural festival designed to celebrate lesbian and gay existence. Unlike activists lobbying for legislative or policy change, Gay Games founders were less interested in reforming the mainstream than in creating an alternative, inclusive model of sporting competition. Although, for many, the Games represented a reaction to homophobia in mainstream sport, significant numbers of participants with little prior sporting involvement were attracted by the principle of inclusion and the promise of community that the Games offered.

Gay Games Organizing and Activism

The first two Gay Games were organized by San Francisco Arts and Athletics, a group founded by former Olympic decathlete Tom Waddell in 1981. By 1989, this organization had become the Federation of Gay Games (hereafter the Federation) and included board members from a number of participating countries outside North America. Gender parity in committee structures was a key principle from the outset. The year 1990 marked the first Gay Games held outside the U.S., with the Metropolitan Vancouver Athletic/Arts

Association (MVAAA), Canada, hosting the event with 29 sports and more than 7,000 athletes. It is noteworthy that the words *lesbian* and *gay* were not part of the names of these first organizing groups, an omission that at least one critic viewed as an attempt to blend into the mainstream (Syms, 1990).

The 1994 Gay Games in New York, with 11,000 athletes from 45 countries, marked the first time that there had been competition between two bid cities; for the 1998 Games, there were three bids, and for 2002, five. The total cost of all five bids for the 2002 Gay Games exceeded the budgets for the first two Gay Games themselves (Boson, 1998), an indication of the growing trend towards emulating the Olympic model.

In the early 1980s when Waddell and others first began organizing the Gay Games, the principle of inclusion had different connotations—different for Waddell, a closeted gay man for much of his athletic career, and for most lesbian and gay athletes. Billy Jean King's experience of homophobic backlash and her loss of commercial endorsements amply illustrated the safety of the closet for competitive athletes. Similarly, jobs in coaching, sport administration and physical education were in jeopardy if sport leaders' lesbian or gay identities became public knowledge, while athletes at every level risked harassment and ostracism if they came out. Twenty years later, with sport still representing the last bastion of sexism and homophobia, legislative and policy changes are addressing some—but certainly not all—of the problems of discrimination facing lesbian and gay athletes.

Gay Games founders sought to provide an opportunity to participate in an openly lesbian and gay sport festival. As Waddell explained, "[T]he message of these games goes beyond validating our culture. They were conceived as a new idea in the meaning of sport based on inclusion rather than exclusion" (cited in Coe, 1986; 7). He envisioned the Gay Games as a way of raising consciousness and enlightening people both outside and inside lesbian and gay communities (Messner,

1984). Participation in the Games would challenge homophobia in the heterosexual world, and sexism, ageism, racism and nationalism among lesbian and gay people. He hoped that his dream of an "exemplary community" would be achieved through inclusive policies and practices: age-group competition, recruitment and outreach to ethnic minority athletes and those from the developing countries, and social and cultural events to break down the barriers of gender, class, ethnicity and dis/ability among gays and lesbians. Two decades later, there are continuing debates about the realization of these goals.

Media Representations of the Gay Games

In most written accounts of the Gay Games, lesbian and gay commentators seemed just as eager as their non-gay allies to *normalize* this sporting spectacle and its participants. There was a consistent emphasis on similarity rather than difference: "We" (lesbian and gay athletes) can break "their" (heterosexual) records; we can organize events that are officially approved by their international federations; and we can produce one of the biggest international sporting spectacles in the world.

In the extensive lesbian and gay media coverage, there is a clear emphasis on using conventional sporting practices to counter homophobic stereotypes and to achieve lesbian and gay visibility and empowerment. In *The Story of Gay Games II*, Roy Coe described them as "an important demonstration of our love for each other and our presence in the world community. Our statement as a minority group was clearly made through the wonderful spirit of camaraderie and friendly competition" (Coe, 1986; 7). And, in the 1990 photo-journal of Gay Games III, the editors stated that the Games

> symbolized for thousands of gay men and women one more step along the road of self-discovery. And for one astounding week in time it was a road they could travel without ever having to

apologize for their existence, or even having to suffer the strain of maintaining an appearance alien to their very nature. (Forzley and Hughes, 1990; 110)

Although the emphasis on empowerment is valid, to reduce the idea to simply "being oneself" and publicly showing "love for each other" is to overlook the sociocultural diversity of lesbian and gay communities. The choice whether to "be oneself" or to "pass" as a member of the dominant group is not available, for example, to lesbians and gays who are Black, or to those who have disabilities. Liberal individualistic notions of self-discovery and self-expression are insufficient for authentic, universal empowerment because they overlook the double or triple oppressions suffered by minority members of lesbian and gay communities. Furthermore, simply bringing together diverse groups of lesbians and gay men in sport does not in itself guarantee "love for each other," and it is naive to hope that sexism, racism, ableism and other entrenched forms of discrimination that divide communities will simply evaporate during Gay Games. On a more grandiose scale, Olympic industry rhetoric calls for peace and harmony, and presents Olympic competition as a transcendent human experience, at the same time ignoring the labour practices and human rights abuses of its multinational sponsors, its impact on low-income and homeless people in host cities, and countless other negative social and environmental impacts (Lenskyj, 2000, 2002a).

Although lesbian and gay community newspapers are an obvious forum for Gay Games debate, they face competing pressures. On one hand, they are expected to generate support for upcoming bids and games, to congratulate organizers and participants, and to celebrate the event as a success story in a homophobic world. On the other hand, since they are the most accessible source of analysis and critique of the Gay Games movement, they will fail in that role if they avoid controversy and self-criticism.

A brief review of selected newspaper coverage of Gay Games III in Vancouver shows few differences between mainstream and lesbian/gay media. *Kinesis*, a Vancouver feminist newspaper, published a supportive information article in July and a five-page, mainly favourable report in September; in Toronto, the coverage in *Xtra*, the major lesbian and gay paper, was mostly positive. In both papers, the only serious criticism was reserved for the homophobic Christian fundamentalists who picketed sporting and cultural events, and threw bottles at Gay Games participants. The American lesbian and gay magazine *The Advocate* was similarly uncritical. Mainstream Canadian newspapers, such as the *Toronto Star*, the *Globe and Mail* and the University of Toronto student paper, *The Varsity*, were largely supportive of the Games and critical of right-wing backlash (Brunt, 1990; MP, 1990; UBC, 1990; Vancouver, 1990).

One of the most obvious attempts to support MVAAA at all costs was Esther Shannon's commentary published in *Kinesis*. Discussing some anecdotal accounts of the Games, she wrote the following:

> A friend of mine told me about ... getting a politically correct earful from two British lesbians ... according to them, the Games were nothing more than an appalling white, middle-class North American spectacle. My friend ... knew these earnest criticisms were valid but she kept thinking, "they're missing the point." [Vancouver] Gay Games organizers are at pains to keep "politics" out of the Games ... [They] kept public debate on the Games' shortcomings to a minimum. (Shannon, 1990; 13)

One might argue that, in the face of the right-wing backlash, a public united front was crucial to the success of the Games. However, the naive aim of keeping "politics" out of sport—also a popular notion among Olympic boosters—is especially inappropriate in relation to a sporting event that is by its very nature political.

Rites, a Toronto lesbian and gay newspaper, published some of the few critical commentaries. Anne Vespry, a *Rites* collective member, and Shawn Syms, an athlete, identified a number of organizational problems that threatened the Games' commitment to inclusion and visibility. Syms was critical of the composition of the MVAAA board: seven white, university-educated members, four men and three women (Syms, 1990). Vespry focused on the shortcomings of the cultural events, including access problems for people with disabilities, failure to subsidize tickets for low-income participants, and underrepresentation of people of colour (Vespry, 1990).

Both Syms and Vespry targeted the MVAAA's assimilationist approach to advertising. Its "straight looking, straight acting" board members, they claimed, opted for a "puritan image," and rendered lesbian and gay people invisible by omitting the words *gay* or *queer* from advertising in mainstream media. Although MVAAA might have argued that their low-key advertising and sanitized public image were justified in light of virulent right-wing opposition, Vespry and Syms are persuasive in their argument that the Games' principle of inclusion requires, at the very least, unequivocal solidarity with openly lesbian and gay members of the community, including the large numbers who reject assimilationist strategies (Syms, 1990; Vespry, 1990).

Given the increased levels of competition among bid cities, pressure on community media to limit negative commentary will be especially strong during the Gay Games bidding process. There was evidence of this trend in Sydney's major lesbian and gay newspaper, the *Sydney Star Observer*, which published mostly positive articles and encountered criticism from Team Sydney (the Sydney Gay Games bid committee) whenever it didn't, or when the timing of a particular article (e.g., Boson, 1997b) did not "suit" Team Sydney's purposes. This did not prevent the *Star's* sport reporter, Mary Boson, from writing, among other critical articles, an insightful piece titled "Are we cheap dates?" in which she identified the danger that lesbian and gay organizations like Team Sydney would abandon their social justice agendas in the rush to get government and corporate funding, and in their efforts to demonstrate the power of the (gay male) "pink dollar" to the non-gay world (Boson, 1997a, 1997c). Given the double economic disadvantage experienced by lesbians—as women and as members of a stigmatized sexual minority—Boson's analysis was particularly cogent.

Gay Games or Gay Olympics?

Since their inception, Gay Games have involved a number of sport celebrities and former Olympic athletes, including Tom Waddell, Betty Baxter, Bruce Hayes, Martina Navratilova and Greg Louganis, and the biographies of Federation representatives and bid committee members usually include their athletic credentials (except for those organizing the cultural festival). The liberal notion of lesbian and gay celebrities serving as "role models" appears to hold sway in the Gay Games movement, and undoubtedly their positive examples and personal courage are inspirational to many. At the same time, however, this emphasis serves to entrench the mainstream competitive sporting ethos modelled on the Olympics, rather than to promote genuinely alternative and inclusive visions of sporting participation, where winning is less important than participating.

Research studies on lesbian and gay community sport demonstrate that it is difficult for those who have been socialized into the ethos of mainstream sport to abandon their often unexamined acceptance of competition and the "no pain, no gain" mantra for an alternative model that values fun, friendship and the pure pleasure of bodily movement. Socialized gender differences make it somewhat easier for women than men to embrace a new ethos of cooperation rather than competition in sport contexts (Lenskyj, 1994a). Greater involvement of feminist women in leadership roles would no doubt help the Gay Games movement to achieve its original radical goals. One troubling trend remains: Only 25 percent of Gay Games III and about 36 percent of Gay Games IV participants were women (Verry, 1998). This increased to 45 percent for Gay Games V in Amsterdam, largely as a result of the Women's Outreach Committee and direct marketing efforts.

From 1982 to 1986, Gay Games organizers were engaged in a lengthy and unsuccessful court battle against the United States Olympic Committee (USOC) to keep their original name, the Gay Olympic Games. Ambivalence over the key political question, "Gay Games or Gay Olympics?" was evident when Sara Lewinstein (Waddell's partner) told the press, "The perception has been created that somehow gays hate the Olympics ... we love the Olympics. We just don't like the dumb bureaucrats who run the USOC" (Waddell and Schaap, 1996; 234). She went on to cite the improved sport facilities that would result from a successful Olympic bid.

In light of these early events, it is somewhat ironic that Sydney hosted the Summer Olympic Games in 2000, two years before Gay Games VI. In fact, according to Sydney's Gay Games bid book, most events would be using facilities constructed in the 1990s for Sydney 2000. Equally important, widespread popular support for Sydney 2000, achieved in large part by the Olympic Bid Committee's pressure on the mass media to suppress any negative reports (Booth and Tatz, 1994; Lenskyj, 2000, 2002a) helped pave the way for lesbian and gay community efforts to win Gay Games VI. The Gay Games bid book stressed the excellence of the Olympic facilities, and stated that the New South Wales government would provide these venues either free of charge or with major subsidies (Sydney 2002, 1997; 57). One section, however, presented an unexpected critique of the Olympic Games: "The [Gay] Games' ideals and prominent sporting participants will be used to contrast the elitism of the modern Olympics and to gain [media] coverage in the run-up to Sydney's Olympic Games in 2000" (15).

The Gay Games represent an alternative to the Olympic Games, but they are modelled in large part on an international sporting competition with over 100 years of checkered political history (and, in the late 1990s, a seriously tarnished image; see Lenskyj, 2000). From the outset, Gay Games' winners were named and recognized, medals were awarded, records were kept, and some events were "sanctioned" (conducted according to international federation standards); highly trained and talented athletes whose careers had been impeded by homophobia now had their own "Olympics." Only a minority of commentators problematized these trends.

Conclusion

The issues examined here confirm that tension remains between the radical view of the Gay Games as an alternative, inclusive and empowering lesbian and gay community event, and the liberal goal of mounting an income-generating, international sporting spectacle modelled on the Olympic Games. The key principle of inclusion, particularly in relation to lesbians, low-income people, participants from developing countries, and people with disabilities, is unlikely to be realized if organizers allow the Olympic model to dominate. However, if leaders can maintain an uncompromising political stance on the issues of inclusion, participation and accessibility, the Gay Games movement has transformative potential.

Conclusion

In women's sport circles, while much has changed, much has stayed the same. As was the case in the first half of the 20th century, issues of appearance and propriety, defined according to white, middle-class heterosexual values, are the key to public and media approval of sportswomen. Despite three decades of feminist and lesbian activism, and despite the apparent liberalization of attitudes since the 1960s, lesbian sexuality remains largely "in the closet" while heterosexuality continues to be exploited in the name of selling sport.

In terms of recognition of women's sport as an area of scholarly inquiry, there has generally been more progress in sport sociology than in women's studies contexts. At the community level, sport is more likely to be recognized as a macro-political issue by grassroots groups opposing hallmark events like the Olympics than by liberal women's groups concerned with marketing celebrity athletes and wooing corporate sponsors (Lenskyj, 2002a; 180). Although sportswomen, including some lesbian athletes, now attract more public and media attention than they did in the 1980s, I would argue that sport hasn't changed—rather, women had to change in order to play the game by men's rules.

Pat Griffin's recent book, *Strong Women, Deep Closets* (1998), documents the ongoing homophobic hostility—or, at best, the slightly more tolerant "don't ask, don't tell" climate—encountered by lesbian athletes, particularly in American college and university contexts. In a cogent critique of fundamentalist religious groups, Griffin exposes the homophobic agenda of the Fellowship of Christian Athletes and Athletes in Action, two powerful organizations that are also active on some Canadian university campuses. By characterizing lesbianism as a sin, and by defining woman's place as subordinate to her husband, these groups explicitly promote an anti-gay and anti-feminist agenda that threatens hard-won gains in these areas (Griffin, 1998; 110–31). At my own workplace, the University of Toronto, it was reported that there has been an increase in homophobic harassment in 2002—explained in part, ironically, by the heightened visibility of gay-positive space, programs and student groups on campus (Rynor, 2002).

Meanwhile, religious proponents of a "cure" for male homosexuality continue to equate sex role and sexual orientation, by claiming, for example, that when boys with poor physical coordination fail in sport, they are at greater risk of becoming homosexual as adults (Burke, 2003). In short, sport is still viewed as the route to (heterosexual) manhood, a formula that leaves sporting females in a sexual-identity limbo.

The "apologetic" response in women's sport that had its origins in the 1970s—the preoccupation with presenting a "feminine" (heterosexual) image—is alive and well. The *Toronto Star* provided examples as recently as 2002, when a female weightlifter at the Commonwealth Games assured a reporter that she didn't "look like a tomboy." Other weightlifters were observed to be "deliberately girlish in the details: the dangly earrings, the manicured nails, the swishing ponytails." (DiManno, 2002). And just before the 2002 Winter Olympics, another woman in a nontraditional sport—bobsled—claimed, unhelpfully, that it "empowers" young girls "to see a woman or a girl [athlete] who isn't threatening, who is still a cute girl" and went on to assert that "you don't have to be this masculine powerhouse" (Starkman, 2002).

Backlash to what conservatives view as equality movements having gone "too far" is no doubt a factor in this renewed attention to emphasized femininity and gender differentiation in sport contexts. Among the most extreme manifestations of emphasized heterosexual availability are the ever-increasing numbers of nude calendars, *Playboy* centrefolds and pornographic Web sites that feature internationally known female athletes (Lenskyj, 2003). Amid widespread liberal assertions that these are independent adult women demonstrating pride in their toned, muscular bodies, only a small number of radical critics, risking the "prude" label, have protested this sexual exploitation of women's bodies.

Postscript

In December 2002, while Martina Navratilova was preparing for the Australian Open, Damir Dokic, father of Australian player Jelena Dokic, told a Serbian newspaper that he would commit suicide if he found out that his daughter was a lesbian (Navratilova lobs back, 2002). Martina had the last word: "It's a good thing that I'm not his daughter ... [then again] ... maybe it's too bad I'm not."

References

Adamson, N. (1990). Sexual Harassment Education, Counselling and Complaint Office, Annual Report. *University of Toronto Bulletin* (October 9), S1–S4.

Adelman, M. (Ed.) (1986). *Long Time Passing: Lives of Older Lesbians.* Boston: Alyson.

Alguire, J. (1988). *All Out.* Norwich, VT: New Victoria Publishers.

Allison, M. (1991). Role conflict and the female athlete: Preoccupation with little grounding. *Journal of Applied Sport Psychology, 3,* 49–60.

Anderson, J., and Nieberding, R. (1989). *In Every Classroom: The Report of the President's Select Committee for Lesbian and Gay Concerns.* New Brunswick, NJ: Rutgers University Press.

Anonymous (1986). In M. Adelman (Ed.), *Long Time Passing: Lives of Older Lesbians* (pp. 64–70). Boston: Alyson.

Antoft, S. (1989). Finding an empowering image of women in sport and physical activity. *Action: CAAWS Newsmagazine, 8* (1), 2.

Auchmuty, R. (1989). You're a dyke, Angela! Elsie J. Oxenham and the rise and fall of the schoolgirl story. In Lesbian History Group (Ed.), *Not a Passing Phase: Reclaiming Lesbians in History, 1840–1985.* London: Women's Press.

Backhouse, C., Harris, R., Mitchell, G., and Wylie, A. (1989). *The Chilly Climate for Faculty Women at UWO: Postscript to the Backhouse Report.* London: University of Western Ontario.

Barron, N., and Lear, B. (1989). Ample opportunity for fat women. *Women and Therapy, 8* (3), 79–92.

Battista, R. (1990). Personal meaning: Attraction to sport participation. *Perceptual and Motor Skills, 70,* 1003–1009.

Baughman, C. (Ed.) (1995). *Women on Ice.* New York: Routledge.

Baxter, B. (1983). Lesbians and sport: The dilemma of coming out. *Kinesis* (July/August), 19.

———. (1987). Out to change the sport system. In Everyday Collective (Ed.), *Everywoman's Almanac.* Toronto: Women's Press.

Bedingfield, W. (1990). Women coaching women's way. *Action: CAAWS Newsmagazine, 8* (2), 8–9.

Bennett, R., Whitaker, G., Smith, N., and Sablove, A. (1987). Changing the rules of the game. *Women's Studies International Forum, 10* (4), 369–379.

Bernoth, A. (2000). Inside Sydney's new global village. *Sydney Morning Herald* (April 11) [www.smh.com.au].

Biddle, S., and Bailey, C. (1985). Motives for participation and attitudes toward physical activity of adult participants in fitness programs. *Perceptual and Motor Skills, 61,* 831–4.

Birrell, S., and Richter, D. (1987). Is a diamond forever? Feminist transformations of sport. *Women's Studies International Forum, 10* (4), 395–409.

Black, D., and Burckes-Miller, M. (1988). Male and female college athletes: Use of anorexia nervosa and bulimia nervosa weight loss methods. *Research Quarterly, 59* (3), 252–56.

Blackman, I., and Perry, K. (1990). Skirting the issue: Lesbian fashion for the 1990s. *Feminist Review, 34,* 67–78.

Booth, D., and Tatz, C. (1994). Sydney 2000: The games people play. *Current Affairs Bulletin, 70* (7), 4–11.

Bordo, S. (1989). The body and the reproduction of femininity: A feminist appropriation of Foucault. In A. Jaggar and S. Bordo (Eds.), *Gender/Body/Knowledge* (pp. 13–31). New Brunswick, NJ: Rutgers University Press.

Boson, M. (1997a). We won! Government goes for gold. *Sydney Star Observer* (November 20) [www.sso.rainbow.net.au].

———. (1997b). Gay Games licence: Sydney hit with $1.4 million fee. *Sydney Star Observer* (December 11).

———. (1997c). Are we cheap dates? *Sydney Star Observer* (December 18).

———. (1998). Games bids "too costly." *Sydney Star Observer* (May 1).

Bouchier, N. (1997). Odd girls on the playing field: The history of lesbians and social stigma in sport. Paper presented at the University College Symposium on Sport and Society, University of Toronto.

Brackenridge, C. (2001). *Spoil Sports: Understanding and Preventing Sexual Exploitation in Sport.* Routledge: London.

Breazeale, M. (1994). The postmodern politics of the lesbian mystery. *The Lesbian Review of Books, 1* (1), 14–15.

Bright, J. (1988). *Sunday's Child.* Tallahassie, FL: Naiad Press.

Brodsky, G. (1986). Justine Blainey and the Ontario Hockey Association: An overview. *CAAWS Newsletter, 5* (2), 17.

Brown, R.M. (1983). *Sudden Death.* New York: Bantam.

Browne, L. (1992). *The Girls of Summer.* Toronto: HarperCollins.

Brownworth, V. (1994). The competitive closet. In S.F. Rogers (Ed.), *Sports Dykes* (pp. 75–86). New York: St. Martins.

Brunt, S. (1990). Inside the gay 90s: the name of the Games is pride. *Globe and Mail* (August 4), A24.

Burke, K. (2003). Catholics push gay-cure tour, critics lash "harmful effect." *Sydney Morning Herald* (January 29) [www.smh.com.au].

Burke, P. (1996). *Gender Shock.* New York: Anchor Books.

Burroughs, A., Ashburn, L., and Seebohm, L. (1995). "Add sex and stir": Homophobic coverage of women's cricket in Australia. *Sporting Traditions, 12* (5), 27–46.

Cahn, S. (1994). *Coming On Strong.* New York: Free Press.

Callahan, T. (1990). Sex, lies and sporting heroes. *Washington Post* (May 27), C3.

Carney, B. (1986). A preventive curriculum for anorexia nervosa and bulimia. *CAHPER Journal, 52* (4), 10–14.

Carroll, J. (1995). Butch babes in trouble again. *San Francisco Chronicle* (May 15), E8.

Carson, S., and Horvath, B. (1991). Sea changes: Jenifer Levin's *Water Dancer* and the sociobiology of gender. *Aethlon, 9* (1), 37–48.

CBC. *Fifth Estate.* (1993, November 2).

Chelladurai, P., and Arnott, M. (1985). Decision styles in coaching: Preferences of basketball players. *Research Quarterly, 56* (1), 15–24.

Christie, J. (1992). Olympic pressure takes personal toll. *The Globe and Mail* (July 23) A1, A8.

Ciliska, D., and Rice, C. (1989). Body image/body politics. *Healthsharing, 10* (3), 13–17.

Clarke, H., and Gwynne-Timothy, S. (1988). *Stroke.* Toronto: Lorimer.

Clarke, G. (1993). Towards an understanding of the lives and livestyles of lesbian physical education teachers. Paper presented to the North American Society for the Sociology of Sport Conference, Ottawa.

Cobhan, L. (1982). Lesbians in physical education and sport. In M. Cruikshank (Ed.), *Lesbian Studies* (pp. 179–186). New York: Feminist Press.

Coe, R. (1986). *A Sense of Pride: The Story of Gay Games II*. San Francisco: Pride Publications.

Cole, C. (1993). Resisting the canon: Feminist cultural studies, sport and technologies of the body. *Journal of Sport and Social Issues, 17* (2), 77–97.

Connell, R.W. (1987). *Gender and Power*. Palo Alto, CA: Stanford University Press.

Corrigan, A. (1992). Fashion, beauty and feminism. *Meanjin, 51* (1), 107–122.

Craig, J. (1995a). CBS stands by Wright. *Boston Globe* (May 13), 69, 76.

———. (1995b). In CBS's eye, Wright wrong. *Boston Globe* (May 16), 53.

———, and Blaudschun, M. (1995). Wright, paper stay at odds. *Boston Globe* (May 14), 94.

Crosset, T. (1989). The abusive coach. Unpublished paper, Department of Physical Education, Brandeis University.

Croxton, J., Chiacchia, D., and Wagner, C. (1987). Gender differences in attitudes toward sports and reactions to competitive situations. *Journal of Sport Behavior, 10* (2), 167–77.

Dagg, A., and Thompson, P. (1987). *MisEducation*. Toronto: Ontario Institute for Studies in Education Press.

Devor, H. (1989). *Gender Blending*. Bloomington: Indiana University Press.

DiManno, R. (2002). I'm-no-tomboy Turcotte golden in weightlifting. *Toronto Star* (August 1), B1, B7.

Dubin, Hon. C. (1990). Commission of Inquiry into the Use of Drugs and Banned Practices Intended to Increase Athletic Performance. Ottawa: Ministry of Supply and Services.

Duncan, M. (1993). Beyond analyses of sport media texts: An argument for formal analyses of institutional structures. *Sociology of Sport Journal, 7,* 22–43.

Dzeich, B., and Weiner, L. (1984). *The Lecherous Professor.* Boston: Beacon.

Eberts, M., and Kidd, B. (1985). *Athletes' Rights.* Toronto: Ministry of Tourism and Recreation.

Edwards, V. (1986). Interview (January 30).

Eskenazi, G. (1990). The male athlete and sexual assault. *New York Times* (June 3), Section 8, 1, 4.

Etue, E., and Williams, M. (1996). *On the Edge: Women Making Hockey History.* Toronto: Women's Press.

Faderman, L. (1981). *Surpassing the Love of Men.* New York: Morrow.

———. (1991). *Odd Girls and Twilight Lovers: A History of Lesbian Life in Twentieth Century America.* New York: Columbia University Press.

Federation of Gay Games. (1997). The Purpose [www.gaygames.org].

Fein, S. (1984). Running defensively. *Ms.* (November), 25.

Felshin, J. (1973). The dialectics of women and sport. In E. Gerber, J. Felshin, P. Berlin, and W. Wyrick (Eds.), *The American Woman in Sport* (pp. 179–210). Reading, MA: Addison-Wesley.

Ferrante, K. (1996). Baseball and the social construction of gender. In P. Creedon (Ed.), *Women, Media and Sport* (pp. 238–256). Thousand Oaks, CA: Sage.

Finney, P. (1995). CBS puts blame on messenger. *Times-Picayune* (May 21), C1.

Flax, J. (1990). *Thinking Fragments: Feminism and Postmodernism in the Contemporary West.* Berkeley: University of California Press.

Forzley, R., and Hughes, D. (Eds.) (1990). *The Spirit Captured: The Official Photojournal of Celebration '90—Gay Games III.* Vancouver: For Eyes Press.

Foster, J. (1985). *Sex Variant Women in Literature.* Tallahassee, FL: Naiad Press.

Fried, B. (1982). Boys will be boys: The language of sex and gender. In R. Hubbard (Ed.), *Biological Woman* (pp. 47–69). Cambridge: Schenkman.

Fusco, C. (1992). Lesbians and locker rooms: The subjective experiences of lesbians in sport. Paper presented at the North American Society for the Sociology of Sport Conference, Ottawa.

Games girls' fund-raising knocked back by official. (1994). *Canberra Times* (July 21), 1.

Garrett, K. (1993). *Lady Lobo.* Norwich, VT: New Victoria Publishers.

Gondola, J., and Fitzpatrick, T. (1985). Homophobia in girls' sport: "Names" that can hurt us ... all of us. *Equal Play* (Spring/Summer), 18–19.

Grandjean, A. (1991). Eating disorders: The role of the athletic trainer. *Athletic Training, 26* (2), 105–116.

Gravelle, L., Searle, R., and St. Jean, P. (1982). Personality profiles of the Canadian women's national volleyball team. *Volleyball Technical Journal, 7* (2), 13–17.

Green, G. (1994). Different rules for female athletes? *Morning Bulletin* (July 26), 6.

Griffin, P. (1984). How to identify homophobia in women's athletic programs. Paper presented to the New Agenda for Women in Sport Regional Conference, Philadelphia.

———. (1985). R.R. Knudson's sport fiction: A feminist critique. *Arete, 3* (1), 3–10.

———. (1987). Homophobia, lesbians and women's sports: An exploratory study. Paper presented at the 95th annual convention of the American Psychological Association, New York.

———. (1989). Homophobia in physical education. *CAHPER Journal, 55* (2), 27–31.

———. (1998). *Strong Women, Deep Closets.* Champaign, IL: Human Kinetics.

———, and Genasci, J. (1990). Addressing homophobia in physical education: Responsibilities for teachers and researchers. In M. Messner and D. Sabo (Eds.), *Sport, Men and the Gender Order* (pp. 211–221). Champaign, IL: Human Kinetics.

Grosz, E. (1987). Notes towards a corporeal feminism. *Australian Feminist Studies, 5,* 1–16.

Guttman, A. (1990). Eros in sport. In A. Guttman (Ed.), *Essays in Sport History and Sport Mythology* (pp. 139–154). Arlington: Texas University Press.

Hall, M.A. (1981). *Sport, Sex Roles and Sexual Identity.* Ottawa: Canadian Research Institute for the Advancement of Women Paper #1.

———. (Ed.) (1987). The gendering of sport, leisure and physical education. *Women's Studies International Forum, 10* (4). Special issue.

——— (1993). Feminism, theory and the body: A response to Cole. *Journal of Sport and Social Issues, 17* (2), 98–105.

——— (1996). *Feminism and Sporting Bodies.* Champaign, IL: Human Kinetics.

————, and Richardson, D. (1982). *Fair Ball.* Ottawa: Canadian Advisory Council on the Status of Women.

Hall, R. (1968). *The Well of Loneliness.* London: Corgi Books (first published 1928, Jonathan Cape Publishers).

Hamer, D. (1994). Netting the press: Playing with Martina. In D. Hamer and B. Budge (Eds.), *The Good, the Bad and the Gorgeous* (pp. 57–77). London: Pandora.

————, and Budge, B. (Eds.) (1994). *The Good, the Bad and the Gorgeous.* London: Pandora.

Harari, F. (1994). Where the willow weeps unnoticed. *The Australian,* (January 18), 7.

————, and Smellie, P. (1994). Lesbianism in sport prevalent but not relevant, says cricketer. *The Australian* (January 19), 3.

Harbeck, K. (Ed.) (1992). *Coming Out of the Classroom Closet.* New York: Harrington Park Press.

Hargreaves, J. (1994). *Sporting Females.* London: Routledge.

Harris, B. (1994). Sex sells women's sport: Graf. *The Australian* (July 28), 22.

Helmbreck, V. (1995). Mechem, players dismiss comments. *USA Today* (May 12), 3C.

Hodges, M. (1995). Ben Wright's swing at lesbian pro golfers reinforces "don't ask, don't tell." *Detroit News* (May 13), C1.

Hudson, M. (1995). CBS keeps Wright after he denies remarks on LPGA. *Los Angeles Times* (May 13), C1, C10.

Huxley, J. (1994). Sneers, leers but all the girls are good sports. *Sydney Morning Herald* (July 30), 7.

Hyde, J., Rosenberg, B., and Behrman, J. (1977). Tomboyism. *Psychology of Women Quarterly* (Fall), 73–75.

Inglis, S. (1983). Report of the CIAU Women's Representative Committee, 1982–1983. Canadian Interuniversity Athletic Union.

Inness, S. (1993). It is pluck but is it sense? Athletic student culture in progressive era girls' college fiction. *Journal of Popular Culture, 27* (1), 99–123.

———. (1994). Mashes, smashes, crushes and raves: Woman-to-woman relationships in popular women's college fiction, 1895–1915. *National Women's Studies Association Journal, 6* (1), 48–68.

Jaffee, L. (1988). Eating disorders and coach/athlete relationships. *Melpomene Report, 7* (1), 12–13.

Johnson, C., and Tobin, D. (1991). The diagnosis and treatment of anorexia nervosa and bulimia among athletes. *Athletic Training, 26* (2), 119–28.

Johnson, S. (1994). *When Women Played Hardball.* Seattle, WA: Seal Press.

Kane, M.J., and Greendorfer, S. (1994). The media's role in accommodating and resisting stereotyped images of women in sport. In P. Creedon (Ed.), *Women, Media and Sport* (pp. 28–44). Thousand Oaks, CA: Sage.

———, and Lenskyj, H. (1997). Media treatment of female athletes: Issues of gender and sexualities. In L. Wenner (Ed.), *MediaSport: Cultural Sensibilities and Sport in the Media Age* (pp. 185–201). New York: Routledge.

Kavanagh (1994). Let's sidestep the politically correct waffle. *Courier-Mail* (January 29), 34.

Khayatt, M. (1987). Gender conformity in women teachers. Unpublished doctoral dissertation, University of Toronto.

———. (1992). *Lesbian Teachers: An Invisible Presence.* Albany NY: SUNY Press.

Kidd, B. (1987). Sports and masculinity. In M. Kaufmann (Ed.), *Beyond Patriarchy* (pp. 250–65). Toronto: Oxford University Press.

Kidd, D. (1983). Getting physical: Compulsory heterosexuality and sport. *Canadian Woman Studies, 4* (3), 62–65.

Kinsman, G. (1987). *The Regulation of Desire.* Montreal: Black Rose.

Kirby, S. (1983). Letter to Editor. *CAAWS Newsletter, 2* (4), front cover.

Kitzinger, C. (1987). *The Social Construction of Lesbianism.* London: Sage.

Knudson, R.R. (1972). *Zanballer.* New York: Dell.

———. (1975). *Fox Running.* New York: Avon.

———. (1977). *Zanbanger.* New York: Dell.

———. (1978). *Zanboomer.* New York: Dell.

———. (1984). *Zan Hagen's Marathon.* New York: Farrar, Straus and Giroux.

Kort, M. (1982). High marks for homophobia. *Women's Sports, 4* (11), 20–21.

Krane, V. (1994). Speaking out: Experiences of lesbian athletes. Paper presented at the meeting of the Association for the Advancement of Applied Sport Psychology, Lake Tahoe, Nevada.

———. (1995). Performance-related outcomes experienced by lesbian athletes. Paper presented at the meeting of the Association for the Advancement of Applied Sport Psychology, New Orleans, Louisiana.

———. (1996). Lesbians in sport: Towards acknowledgement, understanding and theory. *Journal of Sport and Exercise Psychology 18* (3), 237–246.

———, and Pope, S. (1996). Strategies to confront homonegativism in sport. Paper presented at the meeting of the Association for the Advancement of Applied Sport Psychology, Williamsburg, Virginia.

Krebs, P. (1984). At the starting blocks: Women athletes' new agenda. *Off Our Backs, 14* (1), 1–3.

Lackey, D. (1990). Sexual harassment in sports. *Physical Educator, 47* (2), 22–26.

Lawson, B. (1994). $12,500 award for gay jibes. *Telegraph Mirror* (December 2).

Leering case forces limits. (1990). *Toronto Star* (July 6), 1.

Lenskyj, H. (1985). Some reflections on sport and sexuality. *CAAWS Newsletter, 4* (2), 27–28.

———. (1986). *Out of Bounds: Women, Sport and Sexuality.* Toronto: Women' s Press.

———. (1988). In support of choice. *The Starting Line: CAAWS Newsletter, 7* (1), 6–8.

———. (1989). Combating homophobia in physical education: Academic and professional responsibilities. Paper presented at the Tenth Annual Conference of the North American Society for the Sociology of Sport, Washington, DC.

———. (1990). Sexual harassment and sexual abuse: An issue for women in sport. *Action Newsmagazine, 8* (2), 16.

———. (1991a). *Women, Sport and Physical Activity: Research and Bibliography* (revised edition). Ottawa: Ministry of Supply and Services.

———. (1991b). Combating homophobia in sport and physical education: Academic and professional responsibilities. *Sociology of Sport Journal, 8* (1), 61–69.

———. (1992a). Good sports: Feminist organizing on sport issues in the 1970s and 1980s. *Resources for Feminist Research, 20* (1/2), 130–136.

————.·(1992b). I am but you can't tell: Homophobia and the marginalization of women in sport. Paper presented at the Thirteenth Annual Conference of the North American Society for the Sociology of Sport, Toledo, Ohio.

————. (1992c). Unsafe at home base: Women's experiences of sexual harassment in university sport and physical education. *Women in Sport and Physical Activity Journal, 1* (1), 19–34.

————. (1994a). Girl-friendly sport and female values. *Women in Sport and Physical Activity Journal, 3* (1), 35–46.

————. (1994b) Sexuality and femininity in sport contexts: Issues and alternatives. *Journal of Sport and Social Issues, 18* (4), 356–376.

————. (1995a). Sport and the threat to gender boundaries. *Sporting Traditions, 12* (1), 47–60.

————. (1995b). Out on the field: Lesbians in sport fiction. *Aethlon: The Journal of Sport Literature, 12* (2), 99–112.

————. (1997). No fear? Lesbians in sport and physical education. *Women in Sport and Physical Activity Journal, 6* (2), 7–22.

————. (2000). *Inside the Olympic Industry: Power, Politics and Activism.* Albany, NY: SUNY Press.

————. (2001). The more things change: Women, sport and the Olympic industry, 1900–2000. *Fireweed, 71/72,* 78–83.

————. (2002a). *The Best Olympics Ever? Social Impacts of Sydney 2000.* Albany, NY: SUNY Press.

————. (2002b). Gay Games or Gay Olympics? Implications for lesbian inclusion. *Canadian Woman Studies, 21* (3), 24–28.

————. (2003, forthcoming). Sex and the female athlete: The nudity debates. In L. Fuller (Ed.), *Sex Sport Rhetoric Globally.* Binghampton, NY: Haworth.

Letters to editor. (1982). *CAAWS Newsletter, 2* (1), front cover.

Letters to editor. (1983). *CAAWS Newsletter, 2* (2), 3.

———. (1993). *The Sea of Light.* New York: Dutton.

Levin, J. (1982). *The Water Dancer.* New York: Pantheon.

Levine, M., and Leonard, R. (1984). Discrimination against lesbians in the work force. *Signs, 9* (4), 700–710.

Lipsyte, R. (1995). The key word should be "golfer." *New York Times* (May 28), 21.

Lorde, A. (1984). *Sister Outsider.* Trumansburg, NY: Crossing Press.

Macintosh, D. and Whitson, D. (1990). *The Game Planners.* Montreal and Kingston: McGill-Queen's University Press.

Markiewicz, D. (1995). Oldsmobile sponsorship rarin' to go. *Detroit News* (May 29), 1B, 7B.

Martzke, R. (1995). CBS's Wright: "Lesbians hurt golf." *USA Today* (May 12), C1.

Mathes, S., and Battista, R. (1985). College men's and women's motives for participation in physical activity. *Perceptual and Motor Skills, 61,* 709–26.

McKay, L. (1987). Pink Turf Soccer League. *CAAWS Newsletter, 5* (3), 24.

McLean, L. (1994). Lawrence laments calendar coverage. *The Australian* (July 26), 5.

McNicoll, D. (1994). Politically correct pin-ups take the risk out of risqué. *The Weekend Australian* (July 30–31), 11.

Messenger, C. (1990). *Sport and the Spirit of Play in Contemporary American Fiction.* New York: Columbia University Press.

Messner, M. (1984). Gay athletes and the Gay Games: An interview with Tom Waddell. *M: Gentle Men for Gender Justice, 13* (Fall), 22–23.

———, and Sabo, D. (Eds.) (1990). *Sport, Men and the Gender Order.* Champaign, IL: Human Kinetics.

Metheny, E. (1965). Symbolic forms of movement: The feminine image in sports. In *Connotations of Movement in Sport and Dance* (pp. 43–56). Reading, MA: Addison-Wesley.

Mewshaw, M. (1993). *Ladies of the Court.* New York: Crown Park.

Miller, L., and Penz, O. (1991). Talking bodies: Female bodybuilders colonize a male preserve. *Quest 43*, 148–63.

Mitten, D. (1985). A philosophical basis for women's programs. *Woodswomen News* (Spring/Summer), 13.

Money, J., and Ehrhardt, A. (1972). *Man and Woman, Boy and Girl.* Baltimore: Johns Hopkins.

Moraga, C. (1983). *Loving in the War Years.* Boston: South End Press.

Morrison, S. (1991). The fall and rise of Betty Baxter. *Xtra* (February), XS1.

MP praises Gay Games as "rainbow" of diversity. (1990). *Toronto Star* (August 6), A2.

National Eating Disorder Information Centre. (1988). *Bulletin 3*, 3.

Navratilova lobs back and Dokic cops a serve. (2002). *Sydney Morning Herald* (December 30) [www.smh.com.au].

Navratilova, M., and Nickles, E. (1994). *The Total Zone.* New York: Villard.

NBC. (1995). *The Human Edge: One Nation Under God* (January 4).

Nelson, A. (1987). Eating disorders and female athletes. *Melpomene Report, 6* (3), 9–12.

Nelson, M.B. (1991). *Are We Winning Yet?* New York: Random House.

———. (1994). Paid to play a game. In S. Rogers (Ed.), *Sports Dykes* (pp. 87–94). New York: St. Martins.

Newton, E. (1984). The mythic mannish lesbian: Radclyffe Hall and the New Woman. *Signs, 9* (4), 557–575.

O'Hara, J. (1990). Coaches must walk fine line. *Ottawa Sun* (November 14), 31.

Oriard, M. (1986). Jenifer Levin's *Water Dancer* and the feminist sport novel. Paper presented to the North American Society for Sport History, Vancouver, BC (May).

Ormsby, M. (1992). Gymnastics: Is it all worth it? *Toronto Star* (August 11), C5.

———. (1995). Golf talent should be LPGA's "right stuff." *Toronto Star* (May 18), B8.

Ostler, S. (1995). It's all a plot to make them look like boobs. *San Francisco Chronicle* (May 15), D1, D9.

Overdorf, V. (1987). Conditioning for thinness: The dilemma of the eating disordered athlete. *Journal of Physical Education, Recreation, and Dance, 58* (4), 62–65.

OWIAA (1985). *Philosophy.* Toronto: OWIAA.

Palzkill, B. (1990). Between gymshoes and high-heels: The development of a lesbian identity and existence in top class sport. *International Review for the Sociology of Sport, 25,* 221–233.

Pedersen, D., and Kono, D. (1990). Perceived effects on femininity of the participation of women in sport. *Perceptual and Motor Skills, 71* (3), 783–792.

Pharr, S. (1988). *Homophobia: A Weapon of Sexism.* Inverness, CA: Chardon Press.

Phipers, T. (1995). CBS placed in no-win situation. *Denver Post* (May 16), D2.

Piercy, M. (1978). *The High Cost of Living.* New York: Harper and Row.

Potera, C., and Kort, M. (1986). Are women coaches an endangered species? *Women's Sport and Fitness, 8* (9), 34–35.

Pronger, B. (1990). *The Arena of Masculinity.* New York: St. Martins.

Quirouette, P. (1983). *Ottawa Board of Education Athletic Survey.* Ottawa: Ottawa Board of Education.

Reed, S. (1994). Someone's on the fairway with Dinah. *Out* (June), 95.

Reinmuth, G. (1995). Wright denies saying lesbians hurt LPGA. *Chicago Tribune* (May 13), Section 3, 1.

Resolutions from Workshops: CAAWS AGM Sport and Feminism (1986). *CAAWS Newsletter,* 5 (2), 4–5.

Rich, A. (1980). Compulsory heterosexuality and lesbian existence. *Signs,* 5 (4), 631–660.

Robinson, L. (1990). Beating the pink ribbon syndrome. *Globe and Mail* (August 23), A15.

Rogers, S.F. (Ed.). (1994). *Sports Dykes.* New York: St. Martins.

Rosen, L., and Hough, D. (1988). Pathogenic weight control behaviors of female college gymnasts. *Physician and Sportsmedicine, 16* (9), 140–43.

Rubenstein, L. (1995). Lesbian remarks about LPGA land analyst in hot water. *Globe and Mail* (May 13), A17.

Rumscheidt, B., and Lloyd, B. (1988). A church un-united. *Broadside, 10* (2), 3–5.

Russell, D. (1984). *Sexual Exploitation.* Beverly Hills, CA: Sage.

Ryan, J. (1995). "Lesbians" furor? It's all wrong. *San Francisco Chronicle* (May 17), D3.

Ryman, J. (1992). The high price of success. *Ottawa Citizen* (July 27) 4.

Rynor, M. (2002). Challenges persist for equity offices. *University of Toronto Bulletin* (November 25), 5.

Sabo, D. (1987). Opening the closet door: Some political implications of doing controversial research. Paper presented to the AAHPERD Conference, Las Vegas, Nevada.

Sack, A. (1982). The rights and responsibilities of the athlete as a worker. Paper presented at the North American Society for the Sociology of Sport Conference, Toronto, Ontario.

Saghir, M., and Robins, E. (1973). *Male and Female Homosexuality.* Baltimore: Williams and Wilkins.

Sandomir, R. (1995). "He said, she said," with a twist. *New York Times* (May 16), B15.

Sandoz, J. (1995). Lesbian sport fiction. *Lesbian Review of Books, 1* (4), 22.

Schreiber, L. (1977). Great American tomboy. *WomenSports* (August), 35–44.

Schulze, L. (1990). On the muscle. In J. Gaines and C. Herzog (Eds.), *Fabrications: Costume and the Female Body* (pp. 59–78). New York: Routledge.

Scott, P. (1989). Competition: A facilitating or inhibiting factor in female participation in physical activity. *International Journal of Physical Education, 26* (3), 17–21.

Scraton, S. (1992). *Shaping up to Womanhood.* Buckingham, UK: Open University Press.

Shannon, E. (1990). Can you believe the roar of the crowd? *Kinesis* (September), 12–14.

Shapcott, M. (1991). Effective social change through coalition: The case of Toronto's Bread Not Circuses Coalition. Paper presented to the Society for Socialist Studies Conference, Kingston, Ontario.

Sheeley, G. (1995). Ritts calls lesbianism non-issue. *Atlanta Journal Constitition* (May 19), D8.

Shephard, R. (1978). *The Fit Athlete.* Oxford: Oxford University Press.

Sherlock, J. (1983). The female physical educator in Britain as cultural product and as cultural producer. Sport et Sociétés Contemporaines. Proceedings of the Eighth Symposium, International Committee for the Sociology of Sport (pp. 583–588). Paris, France: Institut Nationale du Sport et de l'Education Physique.

Siegel, L. (Narrator, writer and director), and Basmajian, S. (Producer). National Film Board of Canada (1995). *Baseball girls* [Documentary film].

Simmons, C. (1979). Companionate marriage and the lesbian threat. *Frontiers, 4* (3), 54–59.

Slavin, J. (1987). Eating disorders in athletes. *Journal of Physical Education, Recreation, and Dance, 58* (3), 33–36.

Smith, W. (1994). Good s(p)orts. *Courier-Mail* (July 28), 9.

———, and Hudson, T. (1994). Just not cricket. *Sunday Mail* (January 30), 97.

Somers, F. (1930). *Principles of Women's Athletics.* New York: Barnes.

Stanko, E. (1985). *Intimate Intrusions.* London: Routledge Kegan Paul.

Stanley, L. (1977). Sex, gender and the sociology of leisure. Paper presented to the Leisure Studies Association International Conference, Manchester, U.K. (September).

———. (1980). The problem of women and leisure. In Leisure in the 80s, Proceedings. Salford, England: University of Salford.

Starkman, R. (2002). Bobsled's novel personality. *Toronto Star* (February 1), C1, C5.

Sydney 2002. (1997). *Sydney Gay Games VI: Under New Skies* (Bid Book).

Syms, S. (1990). Celebration '90: Physique and critique. *Rites* (September), 13.

Tait, J., and Dobash, R. (1986). Sporting women: The social network of reasons for participation. In J. Mangan and R. Small (Eds.), *Sport, Culture and Society*. London: Spon.

Teskey, S. (1986). Hooked on perfection. *Verve* (August/September), 40–42.

Tey, J. (1946). *Miss Pym Disposes*. London: Peter Davies.

Theberge, N. (1991). Reflections on the body in the sociology of sport. *Quest, 43*, 123–134.

Thomas, J. (1983). Older women. *Running Times* (March), 8–9.

UBC condemns homophobic ad in daily papers. (1990). *The Varsity* (November 20), 7.

Uhlir, A. (1987). Athletics and the university: The post-woman's era. *Academe, 73* (4), 25–29.

Vance, S. (1983). Former basketball coach settles lawsuit against University of South Carolina officials. *Chronicle of Higher Education, 27*, 21.

Vancouver holds the third and largest Gay Games. (1990). *Globe and Mail* (August 6), A7.

Verry, C. (1998). Gay Games 2002—Sydney. *Womensport Australia Newsletter* (March), 14.

Vespry, A. (1990). Reflections on the Gay Games. *Rites* (September), 11–13.

Vickers, J. (1982). *A Comparative Study: Relative Opportunities for Women in the CIAU*. Canadian Interuniversity Athletic Union.

Waddell, T., and Schaap, D. (1996). *Gay Olympian: The Life and Death of Dr. Tom Waddell*. New York: Knopf.

Warshaw, R. (1988). *I Never Called It Rape*. New York: Harper and Row.

Wells, J. (1994). Three cheers for girls with nothing to hide. *Weekend Australian* (July 30–31), 35.

Whitaker, G., and Molstad, S. (1985). Male coach/female coach: A theoretical analysis of the female sport experience. *Journal of Sport and Social Issues, 9* (2), 14–25.

Whitfield, W. (1986). Heterosexuality: A construction of patriarchy. Unpublished paper, Ontario Institute for Studies in Education, Toronto, Ontario.

Woods, S., and Harbeck, K. (1992). Living in two worlds: the identity management strategies used by lesbian physical educators. In K. Harbeck (Ed.), *Coming Out of the Classroom Closet* (pp. 141–165). New York: Harrington Park Press.

Wright no stranger to controversy. (1995). *Chicago Tribune* (May 17), Section 4, 10.

Wrisberg, C. (1990). Gender-role orientation of male and female coaches of a masculine-typed sport. *Research Quarterly, 61* (3), 297–301.

Zipter, Y. (1988). *Diamonds Are a Dyke's Best Friend.* Ithaca NY: Firebrand.

Index

INDEX

New York Gay Games, 137
"no pain, no gain" philosophy, 130, 131, 142
non-conformity, gender-role, 48, 106
Notso Amazon Softball League, 62, 76, 83, 96–102

officiating, 56
Olympic Games/Olympic industry, 29, 56–57, 71–79, 94, 115, 129, 131, 135–137, 139–140, 142–144
Ontario Hockey Association, 69–70

peer influences, 5, 9, 23, 25, 94, 107, 120, 132
Personal Best (film), 63, 129
physical education/educators, 5–8, 11, 15, 18–32, 37, 58, 65, 103–104, 106–108, 110, 111, 121–123, 126, 137
physicality, 90, 96, 98, 102, 112, 123
psychology, 84, 90, 92

racism, 3, 20, 41, 45, 74, 77, 79, 95, 114, 132, 134, 138, 139
radical feminism/feminists, 4, 8–10, 13, 16, 34, 55, 58–61, 70–71, 75
resistance, 39, 56, 84
"reverse discrimination", 39, 45
risk-taking, 35, 90
Rogers, Susan Fox, 108, 118, 133
role theory, 91–95

San Francisco Gay Games, 135–136
schoolgirl fiction, 121, 122
self-defence, 32, 46, 125
self-presentation, 34–35, 48–50, 87–89, 101, 106, 114
"separate-but-equal" sport, 59–60
sex-role orientation, 92, 94, 105
sexual assault, 3, 15–21, 32, 39, 55, 129, 132
sexual harassment, 5, 11, 15–28, 32, 49
sexual orientation, 4–6, 12, 38, 41, 46, 50, 64, 66, 91–92, 104–106, 110, 135, 146
silence, and lesbian invisibility, 9, 17, 19, 24, 38, 45, 64, 66–67, 89, 106, 114–115
soccer, 27, 29, 60, 63, 66
social class, 16, 55, 58
social construction of femininity, 7–8, 84, 90, 92, 106, 112
socialization, 84, 90
socioeconomic status, 77, 113
softball, 8, 29, 48, 69, 76, 83, 95–102, 104, 106, 113–115, 133

sponsorships/sponsors, 29, 43
sport activism/activists, 53–71, 73–79
Sport Canada, 57
sport history, 39, 111, 118
sport literature, 108, 117–134
sport sciences, 32, 83, 84
strength, and sporting achievement, 29, 35, 90, 98, 110, 124, 130
Sydney 2000 Olympics, 73, 76, 143
synchronized swimming, 23, 28–29, 47, 89, 92

team sports, 7, 17, 35, 39, 68–69, 75–76, 91, 92, 120, 123
television coverage/images, 4, 41, 88–89
tennis, 29, 36, 37, 94, 112, 126–127, 132
Toronto, 17, 22, 56, 57, 62, 66, 68, 71, 76, 77, 78, 96, 140, 141, 146
track and field, 39, 63, 94

university and college sport, 5, 15, 17–28, 36, 61
University of Toronto, 17, 18, 22, 140, 146

Vancouver Gay Games, 136, 140
violence against women, 3–4, 9, 11, 16–18, 20, 23, 32, 47, 54–55, 70, 75, 95, 115, 127, 132, 134
volleyball, 60, 77, 88, 95

Waddell, Tom, 136–137, 142–143
winning, win-at-all-costs attitude, 25, 54, 78, 86, 96, 126, 130–131, 134, 142
Women Active in Sport Administration (WASA), 58, 69
women's health issues, 29, 31, 54, 110, 120, 123
Women's Legal Education and Action Fund (LEAF), 70
Wright, Ben, 34, 41–43

youth, and sport, 78, 123

Zipter, Yvonne, 113, 133

173

About the Author

HELEN JEFFERSON LENSKYJ was born and raised in Sydney, Australia, where she gained her teaching diploma in early childhood education. She has lived in Toronto since 1966, and completed her BA, MA, and PhD at the University of Toronto.

Helen investigated immigrant girls' education for her MA thesis, and later changed focus to look at the history of girls' physical education for her doctoral dissertation. Since 1980, equity issues in girls' and women's sport have been her major interest as both a researcher and a feminist activist.

More recently, her political activities have broadened to encompass the negative impacts of the Olympics on host cities and countries, particularly in relation to housing and homelessness, as documented in her two most recent books, *Inside the Olympic Industry* (2000) and *The Best Olympics Ever?* (2002). Since 1998, she has been a member of the Toronto anti-Olympic coalition, Bread Not Circuses.

A late bloomer in the area of sport, she took up cycling, jogging and martial arts when she was in her thirties, softball in her forties, and swimming at age fifty.